QAR

A Simple Taxonomy of Questions

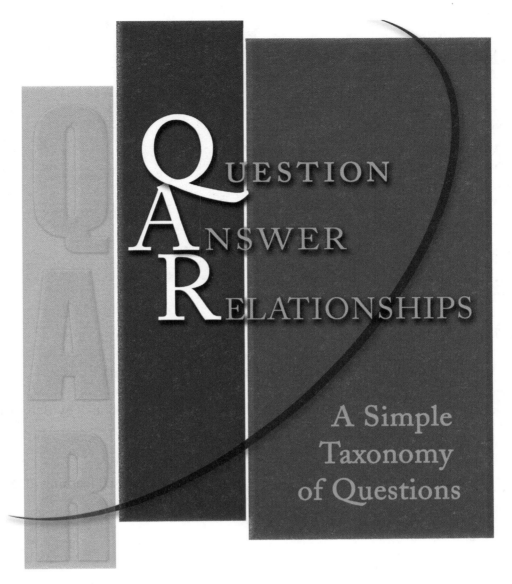

Question Answer Relationships

A Simple Taxonomy of Questions

by Betty Hollas

with Char Forsten, Jim Grant & Laureen Reynolds

Crystal Springs
BOOKS

A division of SDE Staff Development for EDUCATORS

Peterborough, New Hampshire 03458

Published by Crystal Springs Books
A division of Staff Development for Educators (SDE)
10 Sharon Road, PO Box 500
Peterborough, NH 03458
1-800-321-0401
www.crystalsprings.com
www.sde.com

Published 2008
Printed in the United States of America
12 11 10 09 08   1 2 3 4 5

ISBN: 978-1-934026-08-3

Library of Congress Cataloging-in-Publication Data

Question -answer relationships : a simple taxonomy of questions / by Betty Hollas ...[et al.].
    p. cm.
  Includes index.
  ISBN 978-1-934026-08-3
  1. Reading comprehension. 2. Questioning. 3. Inquiry-based learning. I. Hollas, Betty,
    1948-
  LB1573.7.Q45 2008
  372.47--dc22

                    2007047187

Editor: Sandra Taylor
Art Director and Designer: Soosen Dunholter
Production Coordinator: Deborah Fredericks
Illustrated by: JOYCE DESIGNS, pages 36 (top), 53,100
          Marci McAdam, pages 20, 22–24, 36 (bottom), 38 (top)

Acknowledgments

"Individual Achievement," page 59, "Unusual Sports," page 62, and "Team Sports," pages 73–74: From *Sports Math* © 2002 Benchmark Education Company, LLC. Used with permission from Benchmark Education Company, LLC. All rights reserved.

"What Is the Red Cross?" and "How Does the Red Cross Help in a War?", page 63: From *The Red Cross* © 2007 Benchmark Education Company, LLC. Used with permission from Benchmark Education Company, LLC. All rights reserved.

"Florence Nightingale: Pioneer in Nursing," page 67: From *Medical Pioneers* © 2003 Benchmark Education Company, LLC. Used with permission from Benchmark Education Company, LLC. All rights reserved.

"The Arctic: It's Cold Out There," page 68: From *Why Polar Bears Like Snow . . . And Flamingos Don't* © 2003 Benchmark Education Company, LLC. Used with permission from Benchmark Education Company, LLC. All rights reserved.

"It's a Fact!", page 69: From *Building Bridges* © 2004 Benchmark Education Company, LLC. Used with permission from Benchmark Education Company, LLC. All rights reserved.

"The Bhopal Chemical Spill," page 70: From *Ecological Disasters* © 2005 Benchmark Education Company, LLC. Used with permission from Benchmark Education Company, LLC. All rights reserved.

"At School," page 72: From *Colonial Times* © 2002 Benchmark Education Company, LLC. Used with permission from Benchmark Education Company, LLC. All rights reserved.

"Dolly the Doglet Goes Tracking—A True Story," page 56. © 2008 H. Meade Cadot, Jr. Used with permission from the author. All rights reserved.

"The Paper House," page 66: From *Oddity Odyssey* © 1997 James Chenoweth. Used with permission from the author (chenowethj@earthlink.net). All rights reserved.

"Barely Noticeable," page 71, by Polly Pattison: From *Harris Hearsay* © 2003 The Harris Center for Conservation Education, Hancock, NH. Used with permission from The Harris Center for Conservation Education. All rights reserved.

"Rainwalkers," page 75, by Susie Spikol: From *Harris Hearsay* © 2003 The Harris Center for Conservation Education, Hancock, NH. Used with permission from The Harris Center for Conservation Education. All rights reserved.

"Otters Just Want to Have Fun," page 76: From *The New England Naturalist's JOURNAL* © 1979 The Harris Center for Conservation Education. Used with permission from The Harris Center for Conservation Education. All rights reserved.

Contents

Introduction

Whether you are a new teacher or a veteran, you have probably struggled with teaching reading. Many students can decode words efficiently, but still have trouble telling you what they have read. Some of your students come to you with strong backgrounds of experiences that enable them to make connections to text they read. Others come from all sorts of diverse situations that may not include a rich experiential background or even English as a primary language, and they just don't have anything to hang new learning on!

Good teachers have always wanted a high level of achievement for every single one of their students. But not all teachers have access to the tools that make such a goal attainable. Budgetary constraints, administrators who want the latest and greatest reading program (and opt for purchasing rather than piloting), and schools where each grade level functions independently, rather than as a continuum of learning, all contribute to the problem.

In these pages, we offer you a strategy that can translate into success for every student. Thanks to P. David Pearson and Dale Johnson, who introduced the powerful strategy that is the subject of our book, and to Taffy Raphael, who did so much to popularize it, you can teach your own students about question and answer relationships, or QAR.

The QAR strategy is one of the best ways to help students understand that reading requires thinking and that there are different ways to think about different kinds of questions. As consultants and authors for Staff Development for Educators, our goal is to "operationalize" the QAR strategy for you. In this book, we offer not only practical methods for teaching it but also text and pictorial examples, accompanied by the four types of questions, that you can use with your students. Also included are examples *without* questions that your students can use to generate their own four types of QAR questions. Once they are able to do this on their own, you'll see some powerful learning taking place!

Standardized testing challenges many of our students, but especially those from diverse backgrounds. English language learners, students with learning disabilities, and those who lack a rich background of experience, among others, stand to make great gains when they have a strategy that works. With QAR, you'll give these students a practical and realistic way to handle the demands of standardized tests. They will practice QAR with functional literacy—a large part of current testing—as well as traditional academic text. Teaching them to apply the QAR strategy across the curriculum is much more effective than trying to teach to the test—the bar will continue to be raised, after all—and these students need access to a rich and full curriculum if we are going to narrow the literacy gap. When you teach students to focus on and to understand the demands of questions, you give them tools for approaching all kinds of testing situations with greater confidence. QAR will help your students become strategic test-takers with the skills to tackle even inferential questions because they will understand how the construct of the question relates to where the answer will be found.

And there's more good news. Designed to transfer across the curriculum, the QAR strategy can be used by your students throughout their entire school day. They will be able to use it to answer questions in math, social studies, science, history, and other classes because it can be applied to all of their reading.

We're excited to offer this resource to you. Happy questioning!

CHAPTER 1

What the Research Says About Questions

Teachers ask many questions, even more than their students do. Certainly, questions have an important function in the classroom. We ask our students questions so we can figure out what they know and what they don't know. We ask questions to help students make connections between what they already know and what they need to know. In fact, research has established important links between effective questioning by teachers and effective learning by students.

Since the days of Socrates, teachers have always asked questions, whether formally in teacher-made assessments or standardized tests, or informally in class discussions, working with small groups, or one-on-one with students. But have you ever thought about the questions that we ask?

The research may surprise you. Forty percent of classroom instructional time is spent on asking and answering questions—that's for teachers and students combined. Researchers found that teachers ask 40 to 60 questions every hour, and most of these questions are at lower, literal levels of thinking. Furthermore, studies show that it is the teacher who answers most of those 40 to 60 questions per hour, not the students. And when they don't answer the questions themselves, teachers tend to call on the high achievers in their classes for answers more often than on other students. These high achievers consistently enjoy more "air time" than other students do.

Here is what the research has to say about questioning in the classroom.

- Students who ask and answer questions they have generated themselves learn through metacognition. They are actively thinking about their thinking when they can create their own questions.

- The one asking the questions is actually the active learner, so teachers help students learn more when they show their students how to formulate and answer their own questions. In other words, he who asks, learns.

- All students need opportunities to process information at the highest levels they can, not just the high achievers. Students from diverse backgrounds tend to get more instruction in low-level skills and less in high-level thinking skills. Included are children for whom English is not the first or possibly second language, as well as those who have learning disabilities, children who are homeless or transient, children of migrant workers, and those from impoverished homes, and others. We do not have much control over our students' background experiences, but we can and must raise our expectations for their achievement, as well as raise their own.

Questions and Literacy Achievement

There's no doubt that all students need to reach certain benchmarks in literacy. Reaching consensus on what these goals should be, however, requires closer examination. In science, history, social studies, math, and the arts, being literate is the key; students must be able to read and write across the curriculum to succeed academically. To participate not only in a democracy but also in a global marketplace, today's students will require more than basic literacy. They must achieve technological literacy for the twenty-first century. They will need to know how to navigate the World Wide Web and how to analyze and evaluate information they find there.

Let's not forget that "little" issue of testing and accountability—teachers are and will continue to be evaluated according to how all of their students do on various state and national assessments.

We do not have much control over our students' background experiences, but we can and must raise our expectations for their achievement, as well as raise their own.

So, what exactly does it mean for students to reach a high level of literacy achievement? According to the National Assessment of Educational Progress (NAEP), the only federally funded, large-scale testing program in the United States and the framework for the NAEP 2009 Reading Assessment, students will have to read fiction, nonfiction, procedural text, and poetry. Moreover, roughly three-quarters of the questions they will have to answer will require high-level thinking skills. These demands, central to the idea of high levels of literacy achievement, are currently measured on both national and state assessments and will continue to be in coming years. Testing is not going away.

What kinds of questions are we asking in our classrooms? The research says 25 percent of the questions our students are now being asked are at a literal level (think of Bloom's taxonomy) that requires them to simply recall, fill in the blank, spell, tell, underline, label, list, locate, and memorize. That brings the problem into sharper focus! We're asking far too many literal questions that do not require those high-level thinking skills.

> *We're asking far too many literal questions that do not require those high-level thinking skills.... Instead of asking students to label, list, match, or name, we need to be requiring them to apply, construct, analyze, revise, and justify.*

If students are going to measure up on these formal assessments, then we are going to need to pay attention to the demands being made of them on these assessments. We need to start analyzing whether the questions we ask our students in class every day are central to this idea of high literacy achievement. Instead of asking students to label, list, match, or name, we need to be requiring them to apply, construct, analyze, revise, and justify. Our questions should be challenging students to use higher-level critical and creative thinking.

To give the problem a face, or several faces, consider the following examples of three students whom you may have taught.

Our first student, Larry Literal, is forever coming up to you and saying, "But the answer is not here!" It doesn't matter whether he is reading in language arts class, science, or social studies; his refrain will always be the same, "The answer is not here!" Larry Literal stubbornly refuses to look for answers anywhere but in the text.

Then there is Doug Disconnect. Doug just searches his own background knowledge or prior experience to come up with an answer. Doug disconnects himself from the text; he gives it no consideration whatsoever in coming up with his response. He does provide an answer; it just doesn't happen to have any connection to the text he's just read.

Here's a true story from a middle school that illustrates the type of answer Doug gives. In a science class, students were asked to name the three parts of the body. Doug Disconnect answered, "the brainium, the borax, and the bowels, of which there are five—a, e, i, o, and u." Answers like that have driven teachers to retire early!

Danny Dodger is a third student you may have taught. When asked a question on a test, Danny just changes the question into one that he likes better and answers the new question—with no hindrance from the text! We had Danny in our building a while back. As part of our state assessment, all fifth graders had to read an informational passage about the Rose Parade. At that time, the answers were all multiple choice, or multiple guess if you prefer. One of the questions about the Rose Parade asked students, "How do most people feel when they attend the Rose Parade?" The correct response was "excited" and there were plenty of clues embedded within the text to show that's how most people felt. However, Danny Dodger disregarded the demand of the question and answered according to how he personally would feel. Reasoned Danny, the parade is on January first, and what do we do on the night before? Well, it is New Year's Eve, so we go to parties and stay up late. I think I would feel tired. Since "sleepy" was one of the choices in this question, Danny filled in the circle in front of that answer and of course he was wrong. These students fail to understand the role of questions in establishing the parameters for thinking as a reader. You probably teach students who remind you of Larry, Doug, and Danny.

Narrowing the Achievement Gap

As teachers, all of us want to narrow the achievement gap that exists between our students who are fully immersed in the mainstream and our students who come from backgrounds of diversity. The latter includes English language learners; students who speak English but have cultural differences that affect their academic performance; those living on reservations or in isolated rural areas; children with special needs, including physical, mental, emotional, or learning disabilities; as well as others mentioned earlier. High numbers of these students often experience more school failure because they lack background knowledge and may have language deficits, high rates of absenteeism, poor health, or other handicapping conditions. No Child Left Behind (NCLB) has asked us to shine the spotlight on these students from diverse backgrounds and to make certain that our schools' curricula are accessible to them as well as to our mainstream students, and that's a good thing!

When you look at the NAEP reading assessment scores for 2005 (see page 15), it's clear that students from backgrounds of diversity are falling behind mainstream students. The average twelfth-grade black student's score is lower than the average score for an Asian eighth grader. The score for twelfth-grade Hispanic students is only one point ahead of the score for white eighth graders. What can teachers do to help these students achieve? How do we differentiate our instruction to help all of our students reach these high levels of literacy we are talking about?

AVERAGE 2005 NAEP READING SCORES

Ethnicity	Grade 4	Grade 8	Grade 12
White	229	271	293
Black	200	243	267
Hispanic	203	246	272
Asian/Pacific Islanders	229	271	287

QAR: One Way to Narrow the Gap

Question-answer relationships, or QAR taxonomy, is a research-based framework for comprehension instruction with the potential to narrow the literacy achievement gap. It is a comprehension strategy that is designed to provide teachers and students with a common vocabulary for talking about four different types of questions. This strategy can help our students learn different ways of thinking about the questions we and others expect them to answer. QAR will also help them generate their own questions, and when students can do that, they become active instead of passive learners. And that is powerful!

It may sound like pie in the sky to suggest that QAR can narrow the literacy achievement gap that exists between your mainstream students and your students from backgrounds of diversity, but QAR gives every student a framework for thinking about different questions. In addition, it teaches them where to look for answers, and knowing where they can locate a response is a big step toward answering the question correctly.

Once students learn to classify questions, they can figure out how to go about answering them. That's where narrowing the achievement gap comes in. If the QAR strategy can do that, then it's really a gift we give our students.

Here is how this book can help.

- We discuss the development of the question-answer relationship strategy and where it comes from.

- We explain and demonstrate how to use QAR.

- We describe a three-step process for teaching QAR to students.

- We demonstrate how to differentiate your instruction and scaffold it so all your students can be successful.

- We explore how to use QAR to frame questions within the reading cycle and across all content areas of the curriculum.

- We discuss the role of QAR in test preparation.

- We offer an action plan so you will be ready to teach this strategy to your students starting tomorrow.

CHAPTER 2

All About QAR

First, a little background: question-answer relationships, or QAR, has been around since the 1970s. Based on the research by P. David Pearson and Dale D. Johnson, it was popularized in the 1980s by Taffy Raphael, who had become concerned about how teachers were asking questions and how students were answering them. She found that when we teach our students that there are different types of questions and different ways to answer each type, their comprehension improves and they answer more questions correctly. In fact, researchers saw students' comprehension scores improve with just eight weeks of practice using the QAR strategy. (Raphael & McKinney, 1983; Raphael & Pearson, 1985; Raphael & Wonnacott, 1985)

Think about this—QAR, a strategy teachers can use to improve students' comprehension, has been around for several decades and it's still in use. Now there's something you can sink your teeth into! How many educational ideas and fads have come down your school's hallways just in the last decade that have been embraced, adopted, and soon discarded? QAR has staying power!

The difference is that QAR has a solid research base; it's been proven to work for students. We can give you three simple reasons why this strategy has endured.

- **Common Language.** The vocabulary of QAR gives teachers and students a common and consistent language for talking about questions and answers. In addition, it provides different ways of thinking about how to answer different types of questions and where to look to find the answers.

- **Organization of Instruction.** The QAR strategy can guide a teacher's modeling of asking questions throughout the reading cycle, that is, before the material is read, during reading, and after students have read the material.

- **Test Preparation and QAR.** Instead of teachers attempting to teach to a particular test, teaching QAR to students can help them understand the demands of questions they encounter on different tests. When students know where to look to find answers, their comprehension increases. Teaching to any test is a recipe for frustration and failure; the bar keeps being raised. Practice-only test preparation won't do much to improve test scores for students from diverse backgrounds because many of these students have not acquired reading comprehension strategies. What QAR can do for them, as well as for the students who are already in the mainstream, is to give them a tried-and-true strategy for answering questions on high-stakes tests.

That common language, or consistency in vocabulary, is something we can use to talk about questions and answers with our students. All students, but especially those from any of the diverse backgrounds we described, benefit from that consistency of language. When the same terms are used the same way over and over, from one grade to the next and in one content area right across the board to all the other content areas, good things happen for all students. So, even though this book is written with grades three and beyond as the focus, if you can get kindergarten, first-grade, and second-grade teachers to use the QAR vocabulary and graphics with their students, you are going to see some powerful things happen. By third grade, students will have internalized the language, and when they can "talk the talk," they'll be able to "walk the walk."

Even though this book is written with grades three and beyond as the focus, if you can get kindergarten, first-grade, and second-grade teachers to use the QAR vocabulary and graphics with their students, you are going to see some powerful things happen.

QAR also offers a framework for organizing your instruction. You will learn the best, most effective ways to model your questions before, during, and after reading any text. Students are going to be able to use this strategy during the entire instructional day because it is designed to transfer across the curriculum. Just as you ask students questions in math, science, history, and so on, they will be able to use QAR in these classes and others to answer questions. QAR is a strategy that your students will be able to apply to all of their reading.

Teachers often feel that they have to "teach to the test" and that can be a source of frustration for us and boredom for our students. Nothing stifles creativity and the teachable moment like "drill and kill." Even worse, it is not going to help those students from backgrounds of diversity; they need real help to narrow that achievement gap—tools they can take anywhere and apply to all areas of the curriculum. They also need a proven strategy that is going to help them understand the different demands of different kinds of questions they'll be asked on various tests, whether teacher-made or formal assessments.

The most valuable aspect of the QAR strategy is that it really zeros in on student comprehension. When our students know where answers come from, their ability to answer questions correctly increases. The emphasis is on comprehension; learning to label the kinds of questions and understanding the different reading strategies needed to answer them are tools you are going to show them how to use and then put in their reading toolboxes.

Let's summarize what the research says about the QAR strategy.

- Knowledge about where answers come from can improve students' ability to answer questions.

- Students maintain their use of QAR strategies over time.

- QAR training with narrative text transfers when students read expository text.

- QAR teaches students that there are different types of questions and that each type requires a different reading and thinking strategy and different type of interaction with the text.

- The emphasis of QAR is on comprehension and not on simply labeling questions as "right there," "think, search, and find," "author and me," or "on my own." What's important is the answers students supply and the sources of those answers.

Level I:	Level II:	Level III:	Level IV:
In-the-Book/ *Right There*	*In-the-Book/Think,* *Search, and Find*	*In-My-Head/* *Author and Me*	*In-My-Head/* *On My Own*

Adapted from the work of Taffy E. Raphael, 1982, 1984, 1986

This illustration provides an overview of the four different types of question-answer relationships. As you can see, Level I questions are those "in-the-book" questions that have answers right there in the text. Level II questions also have answers in the book, but readers need to look in more than one place to find them, so they are referred to as think-search-and-find questions. Level III or "in-my-head" questions require more of our students; they have to take what the author says and combine that with what they already know to answer this type of author-and-me question. Level IV questions are also "in-my-head" questions. But they do not require any input from the text whatsoever; a student can answer these without reading at all, so they are referred to as on-my-own questions.

Level I: In-the-Book Questions

Right There

Taffy Raphael and her colleagues grouped the four kinds of questions into two categories based on the primary sources from which students would draw their answers. The first major source is within the text, or in the book they are reading. Whatever they are reading, whether it's a passage on a state assessment, a chapter in a novel, or their science, math, or social studies text, the answer can be found within the pages of that text, often contained in one sentence and usually easy to locate. Students can point to the answer—it's right there. Some of the same words that make up the answer are often found in the question, and students need only literal thinking to answer correctly.

So if your students were reading *Goldilocks and the Three Bears*, and you asked them, "What did Mama Bear pour into the bowls?" your students would point right to the line with the word porridge in it and give you the correct response. You know Larry Literal just loves these questions.

We teachers sometimes think that when Larry and other students like him answer these right-there questions correctly, we can let down our guard. After all, they have made meaning from the text and have answered the question correctly. We can move on, right? Maybe not. Take a look at this nonsense sentence.

The racked sevors coarsed auckly along the narvine pel.

We can all read that. It makes no sense whatsoever, but we can decode it nicely. Now let's ask some questions about that sentence.

1. What did the racked sevors do? Right! They coarsed auckly along the narvine pel.
2. Who coarsed? You got it—the racked sevors coarsed.
3. Where did they coarse? Correct again! They coarsed along the narvine pel.
4. How did the sevors coarse? Auckly, exactly!
5. What kind of sevors were they? Racked.

Congratulations! Not only did you read that sentence perfectly—you also understood it. You must have understood it; after all, you scored 100%. Let's all turn to page 32 in our math book and look at problem one. Does that sound familiar?

Do you see the problem? What happens to us, particularly in the upper grades, is that we tend to operate by the clock and that bell or buzzer that's about to go off. Our hearts are in the right place, but we have a lot to do and never enough time to get it all done. So we end up asking literal, Level I, right-there questions. And while our students may be capable of locating the answers in the book and giving us the correct responses, they really are not processing information at a high level. They are instead defining, labeling, listing, underlining, and otherwise operating at the lower end of the continuum of thinking processes.

Level II: In-the-Book Questions

Think, Search, and Find

This second type of in-the-book question can be answered using the text, but for this one parts of the answer are found in more than one place, and the parts must be put together to answer the question correctly. Certain words, including pointer or signal words (see page 102), plurals, and conjunctions, often indicate that the answer is in more than one place. You may refer to these already as key words with your students. Many teachers use these signal words in math class when teaching students how to figure out what to do with a word problem. With Level II questions, the words in the question may or may not be the same words used to answer the question. Because students need to hunt around for the answer to this type of question, it is called a think-search-and-find question.

The illustration for this kind of question shows an open book with markers in several places. That's because part of the answer to a think-search-and-find question might be on one page or in one paragraph, while another part of the answer is in a different paragraph or on a different page. However, the reader still needs only literal thinking to get the correct answer to a Level II, think-search-and-find question.

If your students are reading *Jack and the Beanstalk,* and you ask them, "What things did Jack steal from the giant?" your students will need to think, search, and find to come up with the several items Jack took. That plural form of the word *things* should alert students to the fact that this answer will consist of several words or phrases, and they might not all be located in the same place in the text. If a student comes up to you and says, "I know this is a think-search-and-find question, but I just don't know where to search," celebrate the fact that she is thinking! That is what we want—our students to understand that there are different types of thinking they need to do to answer different types of questions.

Level III: In-My-Head Questions

Author and Me

In addition to text being a major source of answers to questions, Taffy Raphael and her associates identified another major source: the student. We call this category in-my-head questions and there are two types.

The first type is a Level III, author-and-me question. The demands of this type of question are very different from the demands of a Level I or Level II question. In Level III questions, the student must read the text to answer the question, so it is still a text-dependent question. In addition to reading, however, the student must use inferential thinking in order to answer these questions. Therefore, she is going to have to use her prior knowledge, schema, or background of experience to compose an appropriate answer. The student must look for clues and evidence within the text to support and prove her answer, but she must also read between the lines because the answer is not stated explicitly (see box below).

So what an author-and-me question asks students to do is to go beyond the text. The answer is not going to be in the passage in the Illinois state assessment or the Texas state assessment, or in the science text, or in chapter six of the novel your students are reading. Students will still need to read the text, however, in order to answer the question. What *is* going to be different is the kind of thinking

A Word of Caution

To "read between the lines" is an idiom and could be taken literally by students for whom English is not the first language, as well as by other students from diverse backgrounds. Be sure to explain this expression to your students. According to Scholastic's *Dictionary of Idioms* by Marvin Terban (1996), this idiom means to discern the true, hidden meaning or fact in any document or action. The dictionary goes on to say that there are forms of cryptography (secret-message writing) in which cryptographers have to read between the lines of writing or read every other line to decode the real meaning of a message. This idiom suggests that sometimes people write or talk in such a way that their true intentions are hidden. If you read between the lines, you will figure out the true, unexpressed meaning.

they will have to do to get the answer. Your students will glean clues and evidence from the text, but they will be required to combine them with what is in their heads to figure out the correct response.

For example, if your students are reading *Goldilocks and the Three Bears,* and you ask them, "How do you think Goldilocks probably felt when she saw those three bears?", the answer is not right there in the text. Readers aren't told how she felt, but they can't know without reading the text. The difference will be in the students' thinking; they are looking for clues and evidence in what the author says and combining these with what they already know, or what is in their heads.

Level IV: In-My-Head Questions

On My Own

There is one more type of question-answer relationship and it is also an in-my-head kind of question. It's called a Level IV, on-my-own question. For this question, your students don't even need to read the text in order to come up with the answer. Your Doug Disconnect will appreciate these questions. For example, you might say to your students, "What would you do if you were on your way to school, just walking along and minding your own business, and a giant started chasing you?" They can answer that Level IV, on-my-own question without reading anything at all. That's why the student in the illustration is smiling. Look, Ma—no book!

Think about that consistent use of QAR vocabulary we discussed a while back. That common vocabulary is one of the nice things about the QAR strategy; it is so much easier, especially for your struggling students, to understand the terms *right there* or *author and me* than it is for them to understand terms like *literal* or *inferential.* Use the illustrations for the four kinds of questions in this book to teach QAR to students; make classroom posters showing the four types of questions as well as the two sources. Better yet, let students make the posters. They'll be more likely to understand them, internalize them, and actually use them if they have created the posters themselves. Use that QAR vocabulary every day. You will be surprised at how quickly students catch on—these descriptive terms just make sense to them. There's no need to include the terms Level I, Level II, Level III, and Level IV on student-made posters, however. Those categories are mainly for your information.

CHAPTER 3

Teaching the QAR Strategy

The best way to teach the QAR strategy to your students is the tried-and-true three-step method—I do it, we do it, you do it.

3 Easy Steps

I DO IT: The teacher defines and models the strategy.

WE DO IT: The students classify the different types of questions.

YOU DO IT: The students create their own examples of the questions.

First, you'll model the strategy for students many times, always letting them listen to your thinking. You'll also define the strategy and each term for them. You can start by simply talking to your students about questions and discussing the two major sources we use to get answers: text that we read and knowledge we have inside our heads. It takes time to clearly define and model this for students— don't rush through this important part of the process!

Second, you'll classify the different types of questions with your students. You want to make sure that they understand the thinking behind the strategy and the four types of questions. Third, ask them to create their own questions. That's when you'll start to see the lights come on! They're really learning when they can come up with right-there, think-search-and-find, author-and-me, and on-my-own questions. At this point, you know they have internalized the strategy and can access it to use with all their reading. Students enjoy doing this and the process lends itself to all the content areas. If you do literature circles in your language arts class, this process of learning to create each type of question is also an effective format for the discussion leader to use.

Step One: I Do It

First, define the four types of questions for your students. Have them create classroom posters showing the four types of question-answer relationships and highlight those terms that all students can relate to:

- in the book/right there
- in the book/think, search, and find
- in my head/author and me
- in my head/on my own

Create bookmarks that show and define the four QARs, and have students use them with all their reading, including science, math, and social studies. That way, the terms are in front of them when you are reading together and you want to classify questions from the text as your students are beginning to learn the process. (Ready-to-use QAR bookmarks are available from Crystal Springs Books: 1-800-321-0401; www.crystalsprings.com)

The best kind of text to begin with (and model) is simple text, and picture books or books written for younger students work really well for this. There are so many to choose from, and lots of them are actually written for grown-ups—ask any early grades teacher or parent of young children for recommendations. Don't worry about using them with students in the upper primary or even middle school grades. (For a list of suggested titles, see page 100.) In fact, many elementary grade teachers turn to books written for children when they are preparing lessons for a topic they plan to teach but may not be well versed in, such as the circulatory system for science or the Pony Express in social studies. These books can be helpful guides as you search for terms students can understand and ideas for making abstract concepts accessible to all learners.

Another advantage to using picture books is that the text and the vocabulary are going to be more comprehensible to those students from diverse backgrounds who will be able to make great strides when they have a handle on the QAR strategy. English language learners

and other students who may have limited language proficiency will be able to use illustrations to scaffold their understanding, especially when the text features figurative language. Use these books in your modeling and for students to practice the QAR strategy. They will allow you to differentiate your instruction and help you to scaffold support to students who need it (see Chapter 4 for differentiating and scaffolding techniques).

Select short passages from easy reading materials when you begin teaching QAR. Use narrative text as well as informational text and use content area textbooks when you can. You'll want to have lots of different kinds of texts represented in your instruction so you can create many clear and explicit examples of each type of question.

Here's an example of how to begin, using the children's book *Dog Breath: The Horrible Trouble with Hally Tosis* by Dav Pilkey. Because it's full of puns and humorous illustrations, it appeals to older students as well as to younger ones. In this story, Hally the dog belongs to the Tosis family. She has really terrible breath, and when Grandma visits and Hally's breath knocks the poor woman out cold, it's the last straw for the Tosis parents, who decide that Hally will have to go.

To keep Hally from being sent away, the Tosis children try several tactics. They take Hally to a mountaintop, hoping the magnificent view will take her breath away. They also take her on a roller coaster, hoping she'll lose her breath, and so on. One night, burglars break into the Tosis family's home, and at first, seeing Hally's shadow cast hugely on a wall, they think she's a fierce watchdog. When they realize she's really a friendly little pup, they greet her and of course she plants a big, wet, smelly kiss on each of them. Both burglars are knocked out by Hally's foul breath, the family discovers them the next morning and calls the police, and Hally becomes a hero.

To model an in-the-book, right-there question, you might ask your students, "What is Hally's problem?" They will have no trouble with this one because they can point to the line with the answer. It's right there in the text: Hally has terrible, horrible breath.

A good in-the-book, think-search-and-find question might be, "What did the Tosis children do to try to solve Hally's bad breath problem?" They will still be able to find the answer to this question within the text, but now they are going to need to look in several places, on different pages, because the children tried more than one thing.

In-my-head, author-and-me questions are more difficult to answer. They are also harder for us as teachers to write. They require a different kind of mental processing and the emphasis is on thinking. For the previous questions, students could scan the text to find the correct responses. Now they have to bring their own background of experience or prior knowledge to the text. For this one, you might ask students, "What made the burglars think that Hally was a big, mean, scary dog at first?" The author didn't tell us why, but in the book you see an illustration of Hally's large shadow on the wall and the burglars being alarmed by it. So students can infer that Hally's shadow frightened the burglars. It's the clue that they will combine with what is in their heads to come up with the answer.

An in-my-head, on-my-own question might be, "Do you have a pet?" or "Do you know anyone who is a hero?" You want to link what your students think about the topic to what they are going to read, so even though we are discussing this type of question last, when you are using the QAR strategy, you will want to ask on-my-own questions first, before having your students read the text. This is going to activate their prior knowledge, or front-load their knowledge, allowing them to make connections to the topic and maybe make some predictions about what they will read. It's a good idea to have a few of these kinds of questions prepared for any reading you assign because every student's schema and prior knowledge are different. What front-loads knowledge for one student may not do it for another student. As always, consider those students from diverse backgrounds who may need more cueing in order to access their prior knowledge.

Here's a short, easy passage to use for introducing the QAR strategy. Examples of each type of question are included, and you can make up more of your own to use with your students.

As soon as she heard the familiar tune, Kendall sat straight up in bed and looked at the clock. She could not believe she almost slept through her favorite moment of the entire week. She leaped out of the bed and pulled on a pair of jeans and an old shirt. Barely glancing at her reflection in the mirror, she quickly pulled her hair into a ponytail. Then she looked in her drawer for her money. "Oh, no!" she exclaimed. "What's happened to the money I had in that drawer? If I don't find it, I won't be able to enjoy my favorite treat. Maybe I left the money in my book bag." Grabbing her bag as she ran out the door toward the street and the truck, she promised herself she would not take a nap anymore after her Wednesday classes.

A right-there question has the answer in one place in the text. So you might ask students, "What did Kendall do when she heard the familiar tune?" or "What day did this happen?" or "What did she look for in the drawer?" For each of these questions, your students can point right to the line or the word in the text and know the answer.

For think, search, and find, make sure your question involves scanning the text to find the answer, which is going to be in more than one place. You might ask, "What did Kendall do to get ready to leave her bedroom?" While students might say that she leaped out of bed and pulled on jeans and a shirt, if they stopped there they wouldn't have answered the question completely. She also pulled her hair into a ponytail. The next word *then* is a key word students should know about; it can signal more things Kendall did to get out of the room. In this case it does; it tells them that she also looked for her money in the drawer. (See Pointer/Signal Words on page 102 for other examples.)

The answer to an author-and-me question won't be found in the text. It is text dependent, though; students who hadn't read the text couldn't answer it. The reader needs to think differently for this type of question; he will look for clues and evidence in the text, but he'll have to combine those with his own background knowledge and experience to figure out the answer. So a question of this type might be, "Where is Kendall going?" Well, "familiar tune" offers a clue, as do "treat" and "truck." Students will need to read between the lines (see box on page 23), using those clues plus what they already know, to answer that Kendall is going to the ice cream truck to buy a treat. You could also ask your students how old they think the character is. Because she is taking a nap after a Wednesday class, she might be in college. That's also a clue for students to use.

On-my-own questions that could be asked to front-load knowledge might be, "Have you ever slept through something that was important to you?" or "Have you ever misplaced money?" or "What is something you look forward to every week?" Any of these would activate students' prior knowledge for this passage and get them thinking about it in terms of their own experience.

Step Two: We Do It

Now that your students are ready for guided practice, read passages with them and together identify the four types of question-answer relationships. After you have modeled the four kinds of questions and students can use the language, start by giving them plenty of short reading selections. Ask all four types of questions and have them identify each question using the QAR common language. Be sure you ask them to justify their answers. Some of the best learning occurs when students start to argue with you and with each other about the questions and what type each one is. If they are talking about them and defending their opinions with the text, you know that they are actively involved in the process. It's that thinking that is so important. They have had opportunities to hear your thinking as you have modeled these strategies for them; now you get to hear their thinking and they get to listen to their peers.

Jigsaw Strategy

Try this cooperative learning activity to give your students practice creating the four types of questions. Divide students into groups of four and number the students 1, 2, 3, and 4. Point out four corners in your room and identify each as corner number 1, 2, 3, and 4. Ask all the number 1 students to stand in corner 1, all the number 2 students to stand in corner 2, number 3 students in corner 3, and number 4 students in corner 4. Give each student in each group a copy of the same text passage and then ask the students in corner 1 to brainstorm and come up with a right-there question, those in corner 2 to brainstorm and come up with a think-search-and-find question, and so forth. Once they've finished, have all groups come together and share their questions with the rest of the class, starting with a right-there and continuing through an on-my-own question.

Share the following passage with your students and then start asking them questions.

Beth sat on the front porch in the old swing that her grandpa had made. This was her special place. From here, she felt as if she could rest all day. From here, she could daydream about starring in a movie one day. Beth sat back and listened. She could hear birds singing and the whir of the saw out in Grandpa's toolshed. Beth's grandpa worked very hard. He made wooden swings for other people. The money he got helped pay for food and other things for her grandparents.

TYPE OF QUESTION	YOUR QUESTION	YOUR ANSWER
Right There	*Where did Beth sit?*	*In the swing on the porch*
Think, Search, and Find	*Name two things Beth did while she was swinging.*	*Rested and daydreamed about being an actress*
Author and Me	*Why didn't Beth's grandparents buy her a plane ticket to California so she could try out for a movie role?*	*Because they can't afford it. I know this because the clue was that they have to use their money for food.*
On My Own	*Where is a special place you like to go?*	*I like to go to the beach.*

Using a graphic organizer like the one above is a great way for students to begin to organize their thinking about QAR. A right-there question for this passage might be, "Where did Beth sit?" Students can go right to the first line and tell you that she sat on the front porch in the old swing. For a think-search-and-find question, you might ask students to tell you two things that Beth did as she sat in the swing. They would see in one place that she rested, but they would need to look further on for the second thing she did: she daydreamed about being a movie star. For an author-and-me question, you could ask them why her grandparents didn't buy Beth a plane ticket to California so she could go to Hollywood and try out for a role in a movie. You want them to be able to identify what type of question that is, and then to tell you the answer. They know from their reading and their experience that if the money her grandfather earned helped to pay for food, her grandparents most likely did not have extra for a costly plane ticket. For an on-my-own question, you might ask your students, "What do you daydream about?" or "Tell me about a special place where you like to go."

Step Three: You Do It

The last part of teaching the QAR strategy focuses on your students creating their own questions. This doesn't come easily for most students; they are usually the ones on the answering end of questions, so it takes practice for them to be able to generate the four types. Remember that questioning is central to the learning process. Answering questions and generating questions work together to enhance learning. You want students to be able to generate or create all four types of questions as well as identify and answer them. They can't do this if they are just sitting there thinking of lunch. They have to be actively processing language and ideas to do it.

Here's an example for your students to use as they practice QAR.

> *One of Mary Ann's favorite things to do is to plant flowers. Every year she plants flowers in her yard. One spring, Mary Ann planted her flowers directly under the roof of her house. The flowers did not get any sun and they died.*
>
> *That same year, she planted some of the flowers close to the porch. When it rained, the flowers did not get any water. They died.*
>
> *Mary Ann also planted flowers in the middle of the yard. There all the flowers got lots of sun and plenty of rain. The flowers bloomed and grew and grew. The flowers were beautiful colors. They were red, pink, white, and yellow. Mary Ann picked many flowers and gave them to her friends.*

In this last step of teaching QAR, give your students the passage and a blank graphic organizer (see page 103) and have them fill it in. You could also have students complete the middle column, writing the four types of questions, and then let them switch papers to answer another student's questions. In addition, you will want to modify the organizer for those students who still need support, so you might either provide question stems for them (see pages 41–43, "Half-Baked Questions and QAR"), or give them the answers and let them write the questions.

TYPE OF QUESTION	YOUR QUESTION	YOUR ANSWER
Right There	*What is one of Mary Ann's favorite things to do?*	*Plant flowers*
Think, Search, and Find	*Where did Mary Ann plant her flowers?*	*Directly under the roof, close to the porch, in the middle of the yard*
Author and Me	*Where will Mary Ann probably plant her flowers next year?*	*In the middle of the yard (got lots of sun and rain and grew)*
On My Own	*What is one of your favorite things to do?*	*I like to read.*

Here's another passage for practice. Distribute copies of the blank graphic organizer (see page 103) to your students and ask them to write a question for each of the four types.

A new neighbor asked me to babysit her kids. When I got to her house at 5 p.m., I found out she had five children, all between the ages of two and twelve. Before the parents left, they told me that dinner was taken care of, and all I had to do was heat the chili in the microwave.

When the parents left, the kids started screaming and crying for dinner. I couldn't even think clearly, so I got out a metal pan, dumped the chili in it, and stuck it in the microwave. The whole thing caught on fire!

After I dealt with that crisis, there was another one! I was trying to get everyone into bed when I heard a noise outside. I opened the front door and stepped out. Just as

I did that, the two boys (ages eight and ten) slammed the door shut and locked it. Since it was a cold January night, I was freezing, and the boys just watched me while laughing hysterically.

Finally, I got everyone into bed and collapsed in a chair. What I didn't know was that the third crisis was happening while I slept. The twelve-year-old twins had tied my ankles together, so when the parents arrived back home at midnight, I crashed onto the floor trying to stand up! I don't think I'll ever go back there to babysit. I don't need the money that much!

For a right-there question, students might write, "What time did the author go to babysit?" or "How many children were there?" or "What were the children going to have for dinner?" Any of these questions can be answered by looking at one place in the passage.

For think-search-and-find questions, they might write, "What went wrong?" or "Describe the different problems the babysitter had." While the answers to each of these questions are still in the text, the reader needs to search for them in more than one place.

For author and me, students could write, "What were the children in the story like?" or "How many years' difference were there between the youngest and the oldest children?" or "How many hours was the babysitter at this house?" All of these require that the reader has read the text, but that won't be enough to answer any of these questions. Some prior knowledge is required for each one, and that knowledge has to be combined with evidence from the passage in order to answer the questions.

Some on-my-own questions might be, "Have you ever babysat?" or "Describe a time when everything was going wrong."

For additional examples to use with your students, see the QAR samples on pages 55–98. Some are accompanied by the four types of questions; others provide text passages or graphics only, so students can make up their own questions. Instead of a graphic organizer, have students use the Question-Answer Relationships form on page 104. This will enable you to determine which, if any, students need to justify their questions.

CHAPTER 4

Teach to Reach All Students

All of your students will benefit from learning to use the QAR strategy, but as we know, they don't all learn in the same way. This is why differentiating your instruction is essential. Differentiation means figuring out ways to change the nature of the assignment or the way you deliver or present information so that all students can be successful. You are not going to "dumb down" the assignment just because some students (and we all have them) are not going to be able to do it as readily as others are. Instead, you are going to keep the same goal or benchmark in mind for every one of your students. You'll simply move some students toward that goal in smaller steps, differentiating your teaching and scaffolding support along the way.

Scaffolding Text

If some of your students cannot read the grade-level science or social studies text, borrow these from a lower grade, copy the passages you want to use, and make a transparency for your instruction. Now you're differentiating the text for students to make it accessible to them, and you are scaffolding support to them by giving them easier text with which to practice the strategy.

Get Kinesthetic Learners Up and Moving

To help meet the needs of your kinesthetic learners, adapt your lessons so that movement is involved. Try using the kinesthetic symbols on page 36 or come up with your own. What's important is to find ways to teach and reach every student in your room, no matter what her preferred modality.

For those right-there questions, we have used the symbol of a pointing index finger, pressing an imaginary doorbell. That pointing finger alerts students that the answer to the question is right there—they can point right to it in the text.

Kinesthetic Symbols

Right There:

Think, Search, and Find:

Author and Me:

On My Own:

A good symbol for think-search-and-find questions is, of course, the magnifying glass. Students pretend they are holding the handle of the glass and looking through it, searching for answers. They can be Sherlock Holmes, hot on the trail of the correct answers to think-search-and-find questions, and they'll remember that just like a detective, they must search in more than one place. The magnifying glass reminds them to look carefully and examine the whole text to answer these questions. The answer will be in the text, but it's going to be in more than one place.

For author-and-me questions, have students hold their hands together to represent an open book and then point to their heads with one hand. This reminds them that they can answer this kind of question with the author's words, or the text, combined with their own thoughts. They need to read carefully for clues and evidence, but combine those with what's inside their heads—their prior knowledge or background experience—in order to answer the question.

For on-my-own questions, all students need to do is show a big smile. They don't need to read a thing. The answer is in their heads and they can answer the question on their own.

To get your students to practice and internalize these symbols, try this game. Have students stand back-to-back with a partner. You are going to ask them a question and then count to three. When you say three, students will turn to face each other and each one will make the symbol that goes with the type of question that you asked. So if you asked a right-there question, they should have their index fingers pointing to an imaginary doorbell. If you asked an on-my-own-question, the two students will be facing each other with big smiles on their faces. Their goal is to be thinking about the kind of question asked and to each show the same symbol when they

turn around to face each other. You may have done this with other subjects, such as having students make a sad, happy, or worried face to show how a character in a book is feeling when you read them a passage. This game is adaptable to all sorts of topics and nonfiction subjects, and students really enjoy it. It gets them up and moving!

Let's say you are getting ready to do a unit in sixth grade on overcoming obstacles. Team up students and tell them to get ready to practice those QAR symbols. They stand back-to-back, and before they have read a thing or even picked up a book, you might ask them, "Have you ever heard of Lance Armstrong or Jackie Joyner Kerse? How about the baseball player, Jim Abbott? If you've heard of any of these, do you know what they all might have in common?" Then you say, "Make the symbol for the type of question I just asked you." You count to three, and when they turn to face each other, they will all be smiling. They could answer that question without reading a thing. It's an on-my-own question.

Teachers ask these on-my-own questions all the time before students read. It is a way to link what they know about a topic to what they are about to read. We want them to activate their prior knowledge before they open the book and to connect to the text in whatever way they can.

Ask your students to stand back-to-back again, and then read them a short passage, such as this one:

> *When Albert was five years old, his father showed him a compass. He thought about it for a long time, wondering what invisible force kept the needle pointing north. For the rest of his life, Einstein tried to figure out such hidden secrets of nature. The answers he found changed the way we understand the universe and everything in it.*

Next, ask them a question such as, "What kind of person was Albert Einstein?" You count to three, students turn to face each other, and they should see their partners acting like they are reading a book and then pointing to their heads. Why? Because they would need to read the text to answer this question, looking for clues and evidence, but they would also need to think differently about the question. They will have to combine what the author has told them about Albert Einstein (the clues and evidence) with what is in their heads. The text says he thought about the compass for a long time, he wondered, and he tried to figure things out. Most students would know that a curious person might do those things. So it's an author-and-me question.

Suppose you read your students a longer passage from their science text. Maybe it's about an oceanographer who developed a machine to treat water

pollution. Let's say that the text tells you that this man built a series of tanks. The first tank is described in three or four pages, with diagrams and illustrations. Then the text describes the second tank in a few more pages. If you asked your students to describe the different tanks that this oceanographer developed to treat water pollution, and then counted to three and had partners turn to face each other, what symbol would you hope to see them all making? The answer to your question is there in the text, but students are going to need to look in more than one place to find it. So they should all be making the symbol for the magnifying glass because this is a think-search-and-find question.

Here's another one. Read this sentence to your students: "Every year, about 30,000 runners go to New York City to run in the New York City Marathon." Here's the question for your students: "About how many runners run in the New York City Marathon every year?" You count to three again, students turn to face each other, and you see them all pointing to imaginary doorbells. That answer is right there!

Color-Code Questions for Visual Learners

Here's a way to adapt your instruction of the QAR strategy for visual learners. It works especially well with younger children when you are introducing the common language that we talked about earlier. Most students, including second-language learners, are familiar with the color sequence green, yellow, and red in stoplights. You can use that color sequence when you are training students to identify the types of questions in the QAR format. We've added blue for on-my-own questions.

- Green is for go, right? Teach your students that green means they can go right to the answer to a green question. Again, it's right there in the text.

- Yellow means slow down, caution; you'll have to search for the answer to a yellow question in more than one place in the text.

- Red means stop! Those author-and-me questions require readers to stop and think differently. To figure out the answer, they will need to look for clues and evidence in the text and combine them with what they already know.

- Blue is for on-my-own questions. Ask your students to imagine staring up at a beautiful blue sky and just thinking . . . nothing to read!

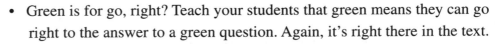

Once students know the color for each kind of question, you can really get into ongoing or formative assessments. One way is to use color-coded cards. Make color photocopies of a set of these cards from the reproducible on page 105 or print out ready-to-use color copies from the CD included with this book. On the back of each card and in the correct location, write the word for the color that is shown on the front of the card (see illustration). Make enough copies so that each student will have a card, plus a few extras in case some cards are misplaced.

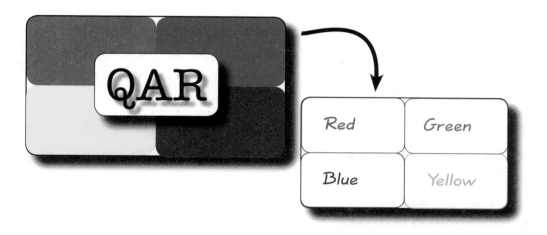

Give each student a card and have him practice placing his index finger on the color that represents the type of question you ask after reading a passage. Begin as always with text they are familiar with already. For example, if you used *Little Red Riding Hood,* you wouldn't even begin with a reading. Go right to the questions. Ask them, "Who was Little Red Riding Hood going to visit?" and see if their fingers are on the green part for a right-there question.

To get an instant assessment of how your class is doing, give each student four index cards, each a different color: red, green, yellow, and blue. When you ask a question such as, "Have you ever seen a real, live wolf?" give them a count of three and see who is and who isn't holding up the blue, on-my-own question card. This way, you can easily determine which students you want to work with in a flexible, needs-based group for extra practice and support.

Colored craft sticks that are the size of tongue depressors also work well for this activity. You can usually find them in red, yellow, green, and blue at most craft stores.

Primary Colors

Using color is a great way to introduce the four types of questions to kindergartners, first graders, and second graders. While teachers at these levels are just introducing the QAR terminology, if the colors and common language are used consistently, by the time you really want to start teaching the strategy for answering and asking the four types of questions, your students will have internalized that language. They will have it in their long-term memories, and your job will be that much easier.

Here's another color-coded activity to try. Arrange students into groups and give each group a short passage to read. Distribute to each student in each group a colored piece of paper; the student who gets a green sheet creates a right-there question on her sheet, the one with the yellow paper writes a think-search-and-find question, and so on. Then students exchange papers by handing their sheet to the student on their left and students answer the question they get. As your students get better at this, you might give them two, three, or all four colors of paper on which to write one of each kind of question. You will hear some great discussions when students disagree about a green question that's been written on a red sheet of paper, for example. And that's okay! If they are talking about the process, they are learning.

Here's the really important part. Whatever you use for color-coding the QAR questions, remember to ask your students to be ready to tell you *why* they think as they do. Why do they think the question that you just asked is a yellow think-search-and-find question or a red author-and-me question? When they can explain their thinking, you know they are on to something!

Scaffolding

Since you will need to differentiate your instruction for many students, we have included scaffolding activities designed to move students incrementally toward the ability to generate their own questions. When we talk about scaffolding, we mean giving students support as they learn each step. They won't "get it" all at once, but neither will they experience failure when you give them support that moves them toward the goal of being able to answer and ask questions independently in the QAR strategy.

Half-Baked Questions and QAR

You can scaffold support to students by giving them "half-baked questions." In other words, you provide half of each kind of question and let them finish the question. You may also have heard these referred to as question stems.

Right There	Think, Search, and Find	Author and Me	On My Own
What? Where? Who? When?	What examples. . .?	What kind of person is. . .?	If you could . . .?
	What are 3 or 4 . . .?	What would you do if you. . .?	Do you agree with . . .?
Define Name	What happened before/after . . .?	What part of the text made you. . .?	Have you ever . . .?
How many . . .? Why does . . .?	Where did . . .? Compare	What will probably happen?	What is your opinion about . . .?

The question stems for a literal right-there question might be

- What?
- Where?
- Who?
- When?

Or students might be able to write a question for this category that begins with the word *define* or *name*. Depending on the text, they could also use "How many?" and "Why does?" to frame this type of question.

With think-search-and-find questions, some stems you might provide for students include

- What examples . . . ?
- What are three or four . . . ?
- What happened before/after . . . ?
- Where did . . . ?

Students might also generate a think-search-and-find question given the stem "Compare."

Those author-and-me questions are the most difficult to write, not only for students but also for teachers. Students will need to refer to the text but also go beyond it to generate these questions. Some stems that might help students include

- What kind of person is . . . ?
- What would you do if you . . . ?
- What part of the text made you . . . ?
- What will probably happen . . . ?

Because author-and-me questions can involve a math operation, as we have seen, other stems might include "How many more," "How much taller," and so on.

And for on-my-own questions, you might provide stems such as

- If you could . . . ?
- Do you agree with . . . ?
- Have you ever . . . ?
- What is your opinion about . . . ?

Schools everywhere have teachers, principals, curriculum coordinators, and others whose responsibility it is to go through their state's assessment after their students have been tested, and actually identify the types and numbers of questions asked at the third, fourth, fifth, and other grade levels. Just as the research shows,

A Word to the Wise!

If our students are being asked more author-and-me questions than any other type of question in formal assessments, then we better ask the same kind of question on our teacher-made tests.

Before you buy commercial publications that are on the market, check to see that author-and-me questions are asked more frequently than any other kind of question. Likewise, if you are asked to serve on textbook selection committees, make a chart and tally how often each type of question is asked at the end of chapters or in accompanying work books or assessment materials. If column three is not heavily represented, we would suggest that you look elsewhere. Remember, these inferential author-and-me questions are more difficult to write, more difficult to answer, and more heavily represented in state and national assessments than the other types of questions.

what these educators are finding by analyzing the tests is that, by far, those author-and-me questions appear more frequently on assessments than do the other types of questions. The students with little or no background knowledge have particular difficulty with author-and-me questions. Like canaries in a mine, they can alert teachers that support and scaffolding are needed for these questions.

When you use the Half-Baked Questions reproducible on page 106, consider highlighting the author-and-me column with bold text, shading, or outlining, so students know right away that the question they write there has to go beyond the text, but must still depend on the text for an answer. Make this column stand out because as we know, these author-and-me inferential questions are the ones students are going to be asked more often on state and national assessments.

Providing question stems graphically in this way can scaffold support and differentiate your instruction for those students from diverse backgrounds. By giving them the first part of the question for each of the four types, you are building a scaffold they can use to support themselves as they move toward independence. Giving students the first part of the question means they are more likely to be successful at finishing each question. And nothing succeeds like success!

CHAPTER 5

QAR in Action

To see how the QAR strategy works and begin to understand it, let's practice. Most students are interested in sports, so we'll use an example from our national pastime, baseball. It's a good one because our students are seeing this kind of functional, real-world text more frequently, along with procedural text like directions, especially on state assessments. Students from grade three on up are being asked to interpret tables, charts, maps, graphs, and time lines, which can be challenging for many of our students. When confronted with circle graphs, pie charts, bar or line graphs, and so on, their tendency is just to pull a number off the chart or graph to answer a question. But when they are taught QAR and they can use it to figure out what kind of question they are being asked, their comprehension improves. Take a look at the following passage and sample questions and try these with your students.

Baseball players and their fans are always interested in batting averages. Batting averages are used to measure hitting performance. To figure a batting average, you divide the number of hits by the batter's official at bats. An official at bat does not include the number of times the batter has hit a sacrifice fly, walked, or been hit by a pitch. So if a player has 10 hits and 50 official at bats, the batting average would be calculated as follows: 10 divided by 50 is equal to .200. Batting averages are always recorded as three digit decimals. Another reason batting averages are important is that they are used to help determine the hitting order of the team. A batting average of .300 or above is considered to be very good in major league baseball.

This Season	At Bats	Singles	Doubles	Triples	Home Runs	Average
Player A	400	65	25	3	4	.243
Player B	397	70	30	3	9	.279
Player C	395	75	36	6	11	.324

Now let's look at four questions, one of each type in the QAR taxonomy.

1. Right there: How is a batting average calculated? (The answer is in one place in the text.)

2. Think, search, and find: How are batting averages used? (The answer is in several places in the text.)

3. Author and me: How much higher is Player C's batting average than Player A's? (This answer is text dependent, but the student must also think differently. She needs to read the chart, looking for clues and evidence in the form of the numbers listed there. However, she then has to combine that information with what is in her head—the process of subtraction—to figure out the answer.)

4. On my own: Describe one of your favorite sports or pastimes. (The answer is not text dependent.)

Our right-there question—how is a batting average calculated—is right there in sentence three of the passage. It is in one place in the text and students can look there to find it.

Our think-search-and-find question for this passage asks how batting averages are used. The answer to that question is in more than one place. Students are told that batting averages are used to measure hitting performance, and then toward the end of the passage, another reason why they are important is given: batting averages are used to help determine the hitting order of the team. The key words *another reason* alert students to the fact that the answer is in more than one place. Notice too that the word *used* appears not only in the question but also in both parts of the answer. We want our students to be mindful of key words when they are reading. (See page 102 for Pointer/Signal Words.)

The next question, author and me, requires students to think in a different way from the first two questions. This question can't be answered just by going back to the text, but students do need to look carefully at that text for clues and evidence. For this question, how much higher is Player C's batting average than Player A's, students must get key information from the table that accompanies this passage: the batting averages for Player A and Player C. Then they have to combine that information with what they already know. Students must know the process of subtraction to figure out the answer. Those students who might have just pulled a number off the chart before would now understand that when the question asks how much higher is Player C's average than Player A's, a different kind of thinking is required to get the answer. And the student's input is needed!

Finally, the on-my-own question can be answered without having read this passage at all.

> *Using the QAR language consistently is critical. When you teach author-and-me questions, you will want to stress the words* clues *and* evidence. *The author will give readers clues and evidence in the text; the "me" part is what is in your students' heads.*

Using the QAR language consistently is critical. When you teach author-and-me questions, you will want to stress the words *clues* and *evidence*. The author will give readers clues and evidence in the text; the "me" part is what is in your students' heads—what they will need to combine with the author's clues and evidence in order to answer the author-and-me type of question.

You can see how this works in the text below about Thomas Jefferson.

In 1801, Thomas Jefferson was elected the third president of the United States. He was chosen because he had already served as governor of Virginia, a member of Congress, secretary of state, and vice president. He served as vice president from 1796 to 1801 under President John Adams. Another reason he was elected president was because he was the author of the Declaration of Independence. He is probably best remembered for the words that have inspired people since 1776—"all men are created equal" and have a right to "life, liberty, and the pursuit of happiness."

Monticello, his plantation near Charlottesville, Virginia, was the center of his world. Monticello included not only a house but also beautiful gardens where Jefferson was always cultivating trees, flowers, vegetables, and fruit. Monticello was also a farm where 150 slaves lived and worked, a 5,000-acre plantation, and a small mountain. Jefferson worked on the design, construction, and remodeling of Monticello for 40 years. Nothing escaped Jefferson's attention as he selected all the furnishings himself. He traveled all over Europe to find many of the pieces of furniture at Monticello. Today Monticello is the only house in the United States designated as a United Nations World Heritage Site.

Now consider the following questions and think about the kind of question each one is. On the line after each question, write the type of question it is, rather than the answer to the question. Is each one a right-there, think-search-and-find, author-and-me, or on-my-own question? Remember to consider the source or sources of answers in each case. Will the answer be in the text, in the student's head, or in both places?

1. Why was Jefferson elected president? _____

2. When was Jefferson elected president? _____

3. Jefferson once said, "Putting up and pulling down, one of my favorite amusements . . ." Why do you think he would have said that? _____

4. Write about something that makes you proud. _____

What did you write for the first question? Students might be tempted to call this a right-there question because of the phrasing in the second sentence of the passage: "He was chosen because . . . ." However, if they scan down further, they will see a sentence that begins "Another reason he was elected president was because . . . ." The words *another reason* will be a signal to the students that they will have to look in more than one place for the answer. It is a think-search-and-find question.

When you do this with your students, it's important to model your thinking process aloud for them. You want to say something like, "Well, that looks like a no-brainer; the second sentence says, 'He was chosen because . . .' and then it tells why he was chosen. So it must be a right-there question. But if I scan further down, I see the words *another reason* in the sentence that reads, 'Another reason he was elected . . . .' So that makes it a think-search-and-find question. The answer is actually in more than one place in the text." Certain words in the passage—*another reason* as well as *because*—are good clues to the answer.

This process of thinking aloud that you do for your students is powerful. It helps to differentiate your instruction and is a way of scaffolding the lesson to support your students from diverse backgrounds as they try using the QAR strategy. All students need to hear our thought processes! With enough modeling, they will internalize the kind of thinking aloud you're showing them and begin to do it themselves.

How about the second question? It's definitely right there. That's the kind of question many students love, but remember that they won't be seeing a whole lot of these low-level, literal questions on state and national assessments. We have to move our students and ourselves as questioners beyond this kind of question.

Question three asks why Jefferson said, "Putting up and pulling down, one of my favorite amusements." What kind of question is that? Does the passage tell us he said that? No, and that's a clue right off that we are looking at one of those higher-level kinds of questions. Were there clues and evidence in the text that would help us to answer that question? Sure! So it must be an author-and-me type of question. You would definitely need to read this passage in order to answer it, but you would also need to think in a different way. What are some clues in the passage about this quote? Well, it says that Jefferson picked out all the furniture himself. That word *remodeling* is a good clue; it sounds like he was never satisfied and was always looking for ways to improve Monticello. There's the evidence; he was always changing how his home looked, always remodeling, and that's what he must have meant by "putting up and pulling down." It took the author *and* the reader to answer that question.

As you read these questions, continue thinking out loud and modeling the discussion that is going on in your own head as you try to figure out a question. All students benefit from this—especially your diverse learners.

Mental Rehearsal

Stop and listen to the thoughts you have as you figure out types of questions, their answers, and the source or sources of the answers. Mentally rehearse the out-loud thinking that you will do to model the strategy. After all, the important thing is not for students to classify questions. The whole point is for them to think!

Many struggling students don't seem to understand that they are supposed to think about the text when they read. They just move their eyeballs across the page; their minds can be a million miles away. We want them to understand that they have to think about what they are reading, and that sometimes they will have to think differently, depending on what kind of question is being asked.

The last question is easy; you don't need to have read the passage at all to answer the question. It's an on-my-own question.

Some of the best learning takes place when your students start arguing with you and each other about questions and what kind each one is. You want that active, involved kind of thinking going on all the time. Collaboration is important in learning to use question-answer relationships because it helps all students process the information and make it their own.

CHAPTER 6

QAR and the Reading Cycle

When you think about any reading that you or your students do, it makes sense to consider it as a cycle with three components: before reading, during reading, and after reading. The reading cycle occurs throughout the school day, across all content areas.

Many students, and probably many pressed-for-time teachers, tend to consider the "during reading" part of the cycle as the meat of any reading assignment. It's easy to see why; it is during reading that teachers find out whether the students are getting it. Can they answer text-related questions? The problem is that many of these tend to be literal, right-there questions that we ask too often, according to the research. With fiction, we may ask students who the main character is and where the story takes place. What is the problem in the story? For nonfiction, we want them to be able to tell us the main ideas. While these questions do give us a sense of whether our students understand what they have read, they can also give us a false sense of security, as you have seen with the nonsense sentence in the second chapter.

To get the most from any text, students need to make a connection with what they are about to read before they open the book. Those who just pick up a book, open it to page one, and start to read are missing incredible opportunities to focus their minds, activate their prior knowledge, ask themselves questions, predict, and make text-to-self, text-to-text, and text-to-world connections. The after-reading component is just as important; it's where the reader internalizes the message of a text and uses high-level thinking skills to process, analyze, extend meaning, and create new awareness. QAR makes reading a contact sport!

Let's think about question-and-answer relationships in terms of the reading cycle. Which kinds of questions are most adaptable to the beginning of the reading cycle, the middle, and the end?

At the start of the reading cycle, before students have read any book, including a picture book, a novel, or a math, science, or social studies text, it is important to front-load meaning. So ask those on-my-own questions to activate your students' prior knowledge about the topic or subject of the reading that is coming. Be sure to ask several of these questions, so that students who don't have a link or connection to one question might connect to another one. Let them discuss the questions you ask prior to reading as well because talking with others will help them to remember information they already know and can now retrieve. Ask them on-my-own questions before you start a read-aloud selection, too, and train them to ask themselves these questions during independent reading time. Ask students on-my-own questions for both nonfiction and fiction text. Remember, the reading cycle happens all day long, across your curriculum, so QAR should, too.

Author-and-me questions are also appropriate at the start of any reading cycle because this is the time when your students look over the book. They check out any illustrations it may have, look for a summary or "blurb" on the back cover, and do anything else short of reading the book that will get them to focus on the

Using QAR to Frame the Reading Cycle

BEFORE READING	DURING READING	AFTER READING
Front-Load Meaning	**Focus and Think**	**Enhance Understanding**
On My Own:	Right There:	Think, Search, and Find:
What do you already know about this topic?	Who is the main character?	Find evidence to support an argument.
Author and Me:	Identify the topic sentence.	Author and Me:
Based on the title, illustrations, or cover, what do you think this might be about?	Think, Search, and Find:	What is the message?
	What are the important events?	How well does the author make his argument?
	What is the problem and how is it resolved?	
	Author and Me:	
	What will happen next?	

Adapted from the work of Taffy E. Raphael, The Reading Teacher, *Vol. 53, No. 3, November 2005.*

text and make that mental or "link-to-think" connection before they read. They are using clues and evidence from the book before they read it to make predictions about the book. Older students who will be reading chapter books should see if the chapters have titles that might help them make predictions about the book.

If the material to be read is nonfiction, such as their science book or a weekly student news magazine, they should read headings, scan for bold-print terms that signal defined words that might appear in a glossary, and look at any graphics, such as maps, tables, photos, and diagrams. This process will activate all kinds of prior knowledge the student has, whether she got it from TV, the Internet, or another book or magazine.

Remember, all this processing has happened in the first part of your reading cycle; students have not yet begun to read. But the wheels in their heads should be turning by now. You should hear crackling and see smoke as they make connections!

During reading, your questions and those of your students will help them to focus on the material and think about it. You will ask right-there questions, like "What year did the Civil War begin?" You will ask think-search-and-find questions, such as "What are the important events that led to the Civil War?" But especially, you will want to ask those author-and-me questions, like "If you were a slave in the South during the Civil War, would you have taken your chances in the Underground Railroad? Explain your answer with information from the text." Now students have to think, process, evaluate, analyze, and defend their response based on information they will have read in the text. You will also want your students to write these kinds of questions during this part of the reading cycle. Think back to Bloom's Taxonomy and you'll see that students are stretching to the top of the ladder of skills now!

When students have finished reading, the goal is to enhance their understanding of what they have read. Ask think-search-and-find questions, such as "What evidence can you find to support this statement: sharks are not as dangerous as people think." Ask author-and-me questions as well. You want students to extend their knowledge and think about what they have read, and to synthesize their understanding to create something new. You might ask, "What

New and Improved!

When your students are reviewing questions at the end of a chapter in their science or social studies textbook, discuss with them the types of questions they are being asked. Then ask them to rewrite the questions to reflect the four different question-answer relationships they have learned about. You'll find that students can often write questions that are better than the ones in the book!

was the author's message?" or for a science text, "In a long period of drought, which kind of animal do you think would have the greatest chance for survival—an omnivore, a carnivore, or an herbivore? Defend your answer with facts from the text."

QAR for Young Students

The International Reading Association (IRA) recommends introducing QAR to your youngest students. To begin using the common language of QAR with kindergarten students, present them with a picture, such as the one below. Apply the four types of questions to the picture. Use the QAR language, but keep it simple. For this illustration, you might ask, "What is the boy looking at?" or "What is the cat doing?" Then say something like, "That's an easy question to answer, isn't it? The answer is right there!" and point to the answer. Young learners will respond to the visual cue of a magnifying glass when you hold one up to an illustration and say, "Hmmm, there is a lot happening in this picture. I'm going to have to think, search, and find the answer."

For author and me, you want to let them hear your thinking as you study an illustration. Looking at the picture of the boy in the chair, you might say something like, "I can see that this boy has a curious expression on his face and that he has been doing a lot of reading. I think he's trying to figure out why a goldfish would wear a bow." For on your own, you might ask them, before ever showing them this illustration, "What is your favorite kind of pet?"

Later, you can move on to pictures where more is happening or use illustrations from favorite read-aloud books, but be sure to keep the common language consistent. Also invite younger learners to make up questions about the pictures you show them. You are building a foundation for thinking about questions and how to answer them. When your modeling is explicit, even these youngest students will understand when you tell them that the two ways they can get answers are from the picture (or the book) and from their heads. They will also understand the terms for the four kinds of questions because they just make sense.

Sow the Seeds for Success

We have been given the daunting task of developing complex literacy skills in every one of our students, regardless of their backgrounds or abilities. QAR has the potential to help us level the playing field for those students from diverse backgrounds who may lack experiential knowledge. With the pressure of high-stakes testing, we can't afford to disregard any strategy that is simple to teach and applicable across all grades, all kinds of reading, and the entire curriculum.

QAR can be incorporated school wide, without huge financial investments in materials that will soon be obsolete. It does not require intensive, ongoing professional development. But you do need to have that commitment in place that all teachers, at all grade levels, including those who teach art, music, computer technology, and physical education, will use the common language of QAR. The language gives students a framework to help them pinpoint their confusion. And when they start generating their own questions about text, whether it is fiction, nonfiction, or functional literacy like menus, directions, or job applications, it is simply impossible for them not to be cognitively connected to the text.

We encourage you to use the text and real-world samples that follow with your students to provide them with even more opportunities to practice this powerful strategy.

Everyone's a Teacher

If you teach in a school that encourages "reading buddies," be sure to enlist your older students as QAR ambassadors. When they are reading with their younger partners, remind them to use the common language of QAR to discuss books with their buddies.

Text Samples With Questions

Dolly the Doglet* Goes Tracking—A True Story

One morning in February, Dolly the Doglet decided to take her people tracking in a forested conservation area in Hancock, New Hampshire. Within minutes of starting their walk over snow-covered ground, Dolly found tiny mouse and—just as tiny— ermine tracks. Weighing less than a quarter of a pound, ermines are mouse hunters that have a white coat in winter. Soon after that, Dolly came upon coyote tracks—just like hers but much bigger. In fact, there were two sets of tracks—made by a coyote couple. February is when New Hampshire coyotes start their families.

Dolly next put her nose deep into a fisher track. This track was even bigger than the coyote track, though a fisher at most is a third the weight of a coyote. This means a fisher can "float" on deep snow without sinking—just like the snowshoe hare. Fishers are large weasels—not fisher "cats," as many people call them—and they eat all sorts of things, from apples to porcupines, but snowshoe hares are one of their favorites. And that's exactly the kind of track Dolly found next. She stuck her paw into the hare's hind foot track, and it was huge! No wonder the name is *snowshoe* hare.

After about an hour, Dolly reached a remote pond on the side of Thumb Mountain, between Lake Nubanusit and the Harris Center for Conservation Education, where Dolly's people work and volunteer. The snow-covered pond was beautiful and dotted with tracks of all kinds. Dolly climbed a beaver lodge to check out tracks and other sign of both another weasel family member, the mink, and one of her own family, a red fox. "Hmmmmmm," thought Dolly. "This track is like mine, only bigger. But it's much smaller than the coyote's. I'd rather play with the fox!"

Finally, Dolly found the tracks of two otters tobogganing across the frozen pond. It looked like they were having fun—and their tracks were fun to follow. But then Dolly's leash broke, which meant they had to head home. And home she trotted, attached to her people by a leather belt one of them had been wearing!

When Dolly the Doglet got home, she had a nice long nap by the warm woodstove and dreamed of all the critters whose tracks she had sniffed and followed.

Dolly's people refer to her as a "doglet" because she is such a small dog. She's a Pomeranian with a big personality—and thinks she's big, too.

Questions

Right There: **During what month do coyote couples start their families in New Hampshire?**

Think, Search, and Find: **Name the different kinds of animals whose tracks Dolly found.**

Author and Me: **What relatives' tracks did Dolly encounter?**

On My Own: **What is your favorite kind of pet and why?**

Rome—The Eternal City

Rome, Italy, the eternal city, is visited by millions of people each year. Rome was the capital of the ancient Roman Empire, and it is also the capital of modern Italy today. It can be very confusing to visit Rome. Many of the streets wind around all over the city. There is a lot of noise and traffic. People often have difficulty visiting the beautiful museums, seeing the spectacular architecture, or getting to their restaurant of choice because it is so hard to move around the city. Another reason Rome can be confusing is that many people do not speak English. So, it would be extremely helpful for American visitors to learn some key words in Italian before vacationing there.

Questions

Right There: **How many people visit Rome each year?**

Think, Search, and Find: **Why is Rome confusing to visitors?**

Author and Me: **What would be some useful words to learn in Italian to make traveling around Rome less confusing?**

On My Own: **Describe a place you have visited.**

Individual Achievement

Gymnastics is one of the most popular Olympic sports. There are many different kinds of events for gymnasts to compete in, such as balance beams, parallel bars, and rings. For some fans, a favorite event is the floor exercise, where gymnasts do jumps, tumbles, and handsprings to music.

Gymnasts must be very strong and very flexible. They must also have an excellent sense of balance.

Most gymnasts begin serious training at a very early age, around four or five. After a lot of practice, some gymnasts enter local competitions. If they do well, they go on to state and national competitions. If they are lucky, they might get to try out for the Olympic team. Only fifteen out of thousands get to be part of the American team.

Questions

Right There: **What is one of the most popular Olympic sports?**

Think, Search, and Find: **What does it take to be a good gymnast?**

Author and Me: **What do you think the life of a gymnast would be like?**

On My Own: **What are your favorite sports to play and/or to watch?**

Flowers and Flags

Designed in the summer of 2002, the gardens at Brad's and Lila's house are an ever-changing palette of flowering plants and fluttering flags. With four rectangular spaces enclosed by a privet hedge, one part of the garden includes some of the original plants from the home's previous owner, who also was a gardener and especially loved daylilies. Plant selections in another part were influenced by a French garden the couple had visited during a tour of southern France. There is lavender, of course, plus other herbs, and decorative grasses as well. And a third part is devoted to the couple's grandchildren, Olivia and Lucas, whose favorite spot is the Play Garden, with its sandbox and adjoining shallow pool where they can wade and wallow around, while rinsing off their sandy bodies.

Aside from the beautiful and unusual flowers and grasses, a flagpole dominates the fourth and final space. This is where Brad displays his collection of more than 75 different flags. The flags are changed periodically to recognize their visitors' home states or countries, the different seasons of the year, a favorite winning sports team, or the name of a family member on her or his birthday.

Questions

Right There: **In what year and season was the garden designed?**

Think, Search, and Find: **What can be found in each of the four different parts of the garden?**

Author and Me: **Do you think Brad and Lila enjoy spending their time with others or prefer to be alone? Explain your reasoning.**

On My Own: **If you had a garden, would your rather grow flowers or vegetables? Explain why.**

Training Whales and Dolphins

Have you ever wondered how animal trainers get an 8,000-pound whale to do a trick? The secret lies in how the trainers communicate with the animals. A good example is to look at how whales and dolphins at Sea World Animal Parks are trained.

The trainers remain very positive with the animals. They pay attention to good behavior and ignore the mistakes. The trainers think that if the animals are having difficulty learning a trick, it is because the trainers are not being as friendly or positive as they should.

Another way the trainers communicate and train the whales and dolphins is by giving them a variety of rewards. Sometimes the animals get fish. Other times they get toys or the trainers rub them and touch them. The rewards work best when they are immediate.

When the animals get in trouble, they are given anywhere from a few minutes to several hours to be by themselves.

Questions

Right There: **How much can a whale weigh?**

Right There: **What do the animal trainers do when an animal gets in trouble?**

Think, Search, and Find: **How do whale and dolphin trainers communicate with and train the animals?**

Think, Search, and Find: **What do trainers give the animals as rewards and when do they give them?**

Author and Me: **What kind of person would make a good trainer of whales and dolphins?**

Author and Me: **What do you think a whale or dolphin might have done to get in trouble?**

On My Own: **What's your opinion about capturing and training whales, dolphins, elephants, and tigers?**

On My Own: **If you could go out to sea in a boat, would you prefer to go whale watching or deep-sea fishing?**

Unusual Sports

Back in 1925, a terrible thing happened in Nome, Alaska. A disease called diphtheria spread through the tiny town. Many children got sick. And the medicine they needed was far away, in Anchorage.

The weather was so bad that no planes could fly into Nome. Instead, people in Anchorage decided to use dogsleds and drivers called mushers to get the medicine there. Twenty different dogsled teams and mushers worked together to deliver the medicine to Nome in only five and a half days.

Every year, there is a dogsled race from Anchorage to Nome to commemorate the bravery of the very first mushers. It is called the Iditarod.

The Iditarod trail runs for about 1,150 miles. Mushers drive teams of dogs across the frozen ground and stop at the tiny villages along the way to eat and rest. It is an extremely difficult race, taking place in a cold, windy, and isolated area.

Winning teams usually take nine or ten days to finish the Iditarod.

Questions

Right There: **What disease spread through Nome, Alaska, in 1925?**

Right There: **What is the name of the annual dogsled race from Anchorage to Nome?**

Think, Search, and Find: **What made this an emergency situation?**

Think, Search, and Find: **Compare the number of days it took to travel from Anchorage to Nome in 1925 to what it usually takes to finish the Iditarod today.**

Author and Me: **What kind of person do you think would participate in the Iditarod?**

Author and Me: **Does the Iditarod involve more people than those who compete in the race? Explain.**

On My Own: **Would you rather ski on snow or water? Explain why.**

On My Own: **What is the worst kind of weather you've ever been in and what did you do?**

The Red Cross

What is the Red Cross?

Have you ever watched the news on TV? Sometimes the news shows a flood. A flood is an emergency. People need help quickly. The Red Cross is an organization. The Red Cross sends workers to help.

The Red Cross helps people in many nations. The Red Cross is international. Does the Red Cross help in your nation?

The Red Cross has many workers. Some workers help in an emergency. Some workers help people before an emergency happens. Some workers are volunteers. Volunteers do not work for pay.

How Does the Red Cross Help in a War?

A war causes emergencies. Soldiers fight near towns. The towns are not safe. Some people leave the towns. These people are refugees. Where will the refugees live? What will the refugees eat? The Red Cross helps refugees during a war. The Red Cross brings tents and food. The Red Cross sends doctors and nurses, too. The tents become hospitals. The doctors and nurses care for the refugees.

Refugees of a war need food, water, and medicine. Refugees need many tents and beds. How can the Red Cross pay for all those supplies? People in many nations give money. The Red Cross uses the money for supplies. The Red Cross sends aid to the refugees.

Questions

Right There: **What are people called who have to leave their towns during wartime?**

Think, Search, and Find: **How does the Red Cross help refugees?**

Author and Me: **Name some other emergency situations where the Red Cross might send helpers.**

On My Own: **Have you ever worked as a volunteer?**

Stormy Weather

A storm is a weather disturbance caused by unusual weather conditions. There are many kinds of storms, but all storms have some conditions in common. For example, all storms start when warm, moist air rises. This rising air results in low air pressure at the earth's surface.

Storms often have strong winds because the pressure near the center of the storm is lower than the pressure outside the storm. The greater the difference in air pressure, the stronger the winds.

The most common type of storm is called a thunderstorm. Thunderstorms have tall clouds, rain, and thunder and lightning. The storm that is largest in size is a hurricane. It is a large tropical storm with high winds and heavy rainfall. Hurricanes form over warm, tropical oceans. When they move over land, they can cause much damage from strong winds and flooding. As a hurricane continues to move over land, it loses much of its energy, becoming nothing more than a heavy rainstorm.

An extremely damaging type of storm is the tornado. A tornado is a violent, whirling wind accompanied by a funnel-shaped cloud that races over land in a narrow path. The strong winds can pick up a house and toss it aside like it is a toy.

Questions

Right There: **Define a storm.**

Right There: **What is the most common type of storm?**

Think, Search, and Find: **What common conditions are found in all storms?**

Think, Search, and Find: **What are some of the more common storms?**

Author and Me: **What do you think is the most destructive land-based storm?**

Author and Me: **In addition to these storms, what other kinds are there?**

On My Own: **Would you like to be a weather forecaster? Why or why not?**

On My Own: **Do you think people should be forced to leave their homes when a major storm like a hurricane is heading their way? Explain why or why not.**

Text Samples Without Questions

The Paper House

In the Pigeon Cove section of Rockport, Massachusetts, you can see a unique house built by the Stenman family in 1922. It took 20 years to finish and began as an experiment to see what could be done architecturally with newspapers. Except for the roof, floors, doors, windows, and fireplace, the house was made entirely out of newspapers—rolled or folded, then glued and varnished. More than 100,000 daily editions were used. The walls are 215 pages thick.

Even the furniture is made of newspaper. On part of the writing desk, one can still read an account of Charles Lindbergh's historic flight. A grandfather clock is made of newspapers from capital cities in the U.S. when there were only 48 states. Magazine sections from the Sunday Boston *Herald* and the New York *Herald Tribune* make up the massive, ceiling-high mantel over the fireplace. A cot is constructed of papers saved since World War I, and the newspaper piano still plays!

❖❖❖❖❖❖ ❖❖❖❖❖❖ ❖❖❖❖❖❖ ❖❖❖❖❖❖ ❖❖❖❖❖❖ ❖❖❖❖❖❖ ❖❖❖❖❖❖ ❖❖❖❖❖❖

Florence Nightingale: Pioneer in Nursing

Today nurses, along with doctors, take care of the sick. In fact, the word "nurse" means "to take care of." One hundred and fifty years ago, nurses did not care for people in the hospital. Back then they swept floors, emptied bedpans, and did the laundry. In the mid-1800s, one woman changed all that. Her name was Florence Nightingale.

Florence Nightingale was born in Florence, Italy, while her wealthy English parents were traveling in Europe. As a child she traveled to many places with her family and learned how to speak several languages.

When Nightingale was seventeen, she told her family that she was going to help sick people. Her parents did not approve, but Nightingale was determined.

She traveled to hospitals all over Europe. She saw that doctors were working too hard. She saw that patients died because they did not get enough care. Nightingale felt that women could be doing more to help doctors take care of sick people.

Nightingale knew that in order for nurses to do more, they needed special training in how to take care of sick people. Nightingale went to a hospital in Germany to study nursing. Then she returned to London and became the head of a group of women called Gentlewomen During Illness. These women cared for sick people in their homes.

In 1854, England was fighting the Crimean War with Russia. War reporters wrote about the terrible conditions in the hospitals that cared for the wounded. People demanded that something be done about it. A leader of the government asked Florence Nightingale to take some nurses into the war hospitals. So in November 1854, Nightingale finally got to work in a hospital. She took along thirty-eight nurses whom she had trained herself.

At first the doctors on the battlefields did not want Nightingale and her nurses in their hospitals. They did not believe that women could help. But in fact, the nurses did make a difference. They worked around the clock, tending the sick. Thanks to their hard work, many wounded soldiers survived.

After the war, Nightingale and her nurses were treated like heroes. Finally, in 1860, she started the Nightingale School for Nurses. In time, thanks to Florence Nightingale, nursing became an important part of medicine.

The Arctic: It's Cold Out There

The Arctic, way up near the North Pole, is very cold. The ground is covered with snow almost all year long. There are not very many trees or plants. In the summer the sun never really sets, but in fall and winter, it is dark most of the time. The temperature in winter is usually about –30° Fahrenheit (–34° Celsius), and it can get even colder. Arctic animals are adapted for life in a cold place. They have some interesting ways of keeping warm and protecting themselves.

One way Arctic animals stay warm is by having lots of fur. Another is by having a lot of fat. Polar bears have both: lots of warm fur and a thick layer of fat just under the skin. The fat acts like an extra layer of clothing to keep out the cold.

Seals and walruses have a thick layer of fat, too. It is called blubber. The thick layer of blubber under their skins keeps them warm, even in the freezing waters of the Arctic Ocean.

Believe it or not, having small ears helps keep an animal warm. A lot of the warmth from an animal's body escapes through the ears. Arctic animals need to keep in all the body heat they can. The Arctic hare has smaller ears than most rabbits. And the Arctic fox's ears are smaller than those of foxes that live in warmer habitats.

Many of the animals living in the Arctic are white. They are hard to see because they blend in with the white snow. Coloring that makes an animal blend in with its surroundings is called camouflage.

Camouflage protects the white Arctic hare from other animals that might hunt and kill it for food. Camouflage helps animals that hunt, too. The white polar bear can creep over the snow and ice and never be seen by the seals it hunts and eats.

The Arctic fox and the Arctic hare actually change color. In the summer, when the snow melts, they shed their white fur and grow a grayish coat. When the snow comes back, their white fur grows back again!

❖❖❖❖❖❖ ❖❖❖❖❖❖ ❖❖❖❖❖❖ ❖❖❖❖❖❖ ❖❖❖❖❖❖ ❖❖❖❖❖❖ ❖❖❖❖❖❖ ❖❖❖❖❖❖

It's A Fact!

New York City's Brooklyn Bridge is one of the world's most famous bridges. Designed in 1869 by John A. Roebling, the bridge was not completed until 1883. Building it was dangerous work. It cost the lives of 27 workers. One of the first to die was designer Roebling. He was killed in an accident during the final planning stages. His son, Washington Roebling, took over.

Crews had to work underwater to build the foundations for the towers that supported the span. So the workers first sank watertight containers, called caissons (KAY-suhnz), to the bottom of the river. These caissons provided a place for the crews to work underwater.

Bridge builders worked long hours in caissons deep beneath the East River. Many suffered because the pressure around their bodies changed too quickly when they went in and out of the caissons. Some workers died.

Caisson disease left Washington Roebling deaf and unable to walk. But he wouldn't give up work on the project! He supervised from his bedroom window in Brooklyn, where he could watch the bridge construction. His wife, Emily, gave orders to the workers for him.

From *Building Bridges* © 2004 Benchmark Education Company, LLC. Used with permission from Benchmark Education Company, LLC. All rights reserved.

The Bhopal Chemical Spill

On the night of December 2, 1984, residents of Bhopal (BOH–pahl), India, were sleeping peacefully. In a nearby chemical (KEHM-ih-kuhl) plant, one of the pipes started to leak. Around 12:17 AM on December 3, gas began to spray from the tank. Terrified workers fled. Huge clouds of gas spread into the neighborhood. The sharp smell of chemicals filled the air. People woke up coughing. Their lungs felt like they were on fire. Their eyes were stinging. Two thousand people died quickly.

Why did such a terrible chemical spill happen? The Union Carbide chemical plant in Bhopal made pesticides (PES-tih-sighdz), chemicals used to kill insects. One of its chemicals, MIC is toxic (TAHK-sihk). It poisons very quickly.

Workers were not worried when one tank began to leak. Small MIC leaks happened all the time. But no one knew that water had gotten into the tank. The water and the MIC formed a highly toxic gas. A safety vent, made to trap the gas, was not working. By the time workers realized what was happening, the gas was spreading throughout the city.

Terrified workers ran away from the direction of the wind, as they had been trained. None of them were hurt. But the neighborhood people had never been trained what to do in case of an accident. They ran right into the cloud of gas.

It was hard to see. People coughed and cried, tripped and fell. Some became very sick. Many people were blinded by the gas. If they had known to put wet towels over their faces, the gas might not have hurt them.

❖❖❖❖❖❖❖ ❖❖❖❖❖❖❖ ❖❖❖❖❖❖❖ ❖❖❖❖❖❖❖ ❖❖❖❖❖❖❖ ❖❖❖❖❖❖❖ ❖❖❖❖❖❖❖ ❖❖❖❖❖❖❖

Barely Noticeable

They're out there. We might not see them, or hear them, but we know they're there. Bears. North American Black Bears.

They're out and about, desperately looking for spring greens, trying to get through this time of lean living until the abundance of new growth can satisfy the near starvation they experience upon leaving their winter dens. And they're not all alone. The sows who bore one, two, three, or possibly four cubs during their winter sleep, now have the occupation of teacher and tour guide, protector and provider for their offspring.

When the cubs were born in February, their birth weight was approximately six ounces, about the size of a stick of butter. When they emerge from the close quarters of their dens in the spring, the cubs weigh around five pounds, after nursing on their sleepy mother, who hasn't had a bit to eat since last fall. No wonder she's hungry!

Black Bears are good parents. The sow will spend almost a year and a half with her young, teaching her cubs to retreat from danger. She also may teach her cubs to access birdfeeders during those food-scarce months of early spring.

It's easy to fall for these creatures. There's something unmistakably majestic about Black Bears. Although they may be the smallest bear in North America, coming in third after the Grizzly and the largest of all the bears in the world—the Polar bear—they are beautiful, powerful, and elusive. They're playful, curious, intelligent. They climb trees, and swim to escape the summer heat. They avoid danger and try to sound scary when they're frightened.

Black bears are a lot like us. And they're out there, right now, keeping out of sight, climbing the slopes, trying to get by, just like the rest of us.

At School

Not all children went to school. Those who did started in what was called a dame school. The teacher of a dame school was a woman. Children went to her house to learn to read and write. Because books were very expensive, young children often learned their letters from a hornbook. A hornbook was a piece of wood with the alphabet on one side and usually a story on the other side. When children could read on both sides of the hornbook, they were finished with dame school.

Towns with more than fifty families were required to build common schools so that boys could continue their education. In some colonies, girls could attend common school, too. In others, they stayed home and learned household duties.

Common schools had only one room. During the cold winter, a single fireplace provided the only heat. Every student had to bring in wood for the fire. If a student did not bring wood, he had to sit far from the fire's warmth.

The common-school teachers were usually men. Students' families were responsible for paying the teacher, who was called the schoolmaster. Some families paid with money. Others paid with food supplies.

The only schoolbook was the *New-England Primer*. It used prayers and rhymes to teach the letters of the alphabet.

Paper was expensive, so the students wrote on peelings of birch bark. They wrote with lumps of lead or used goose-feather pens dipped in homemade ink.

Schoolmasters were strict. If a student wasn't paying attention, the schoolmaster might hang a sign around his neck that read "Idle Boy." A student who didn't know his lessons would have to sit on a dunce stool and wear a dunce cap.

At the age of eleven, when most boys finished their studies, they went to work. However, boys from wealthy families often had private tutors and went to college.

TEXT SAMPLES

Team Sports

People love to play and watch team sports. One of the most popular team sports is baseball.

Some baseball fans are really into numbers. They can tell you how many times a player has struck out, how many games a team has won, and even how many home runs have been hit in a particular baseball park. More than anything else, though, baseball fans seem to enjoy arguing over who the greatest baseball player of all time was. A strong batter? A fast runner? A good fielder? An awesome pitcher? What do you think?

One way to pick a baseball great is to look at the player's batting average. A batting average tells how often a player gets a hit compared to how often he bats.

Hitting a ball in the major leagues is harder than you might think. Baseball great Ted Williams once said that the best players hit the ball only three out of every ten times at bat!

Football is one of the great American sports. Some people think that football began back in the 1860s, when college students played a new version of rugby. Both football and rugby are games in which players have to get the ball into the goal by running with it, throwing it, and kicking it.

Ever since the first football game was played, fans have been coming out to watch their teams compete. While high school fields might have room for only 100 fans, college and professional teams have room for thousands of people.

Most teams keep track of attendance at each game. Attendance is the number of fans who come to watch the game. Does each team send out a person to count all of the seats? Probably not. Instead, officials keep track of how many tickets are sold.

It is said that basketball was invented in Massachusetts on a cold winter day back in 1891. A teacher named James Naismith wanted to invent a team sport that his students could play inside. He got a soccer ball and hung two peach baskets at either end of the gym. During that very first game, Naismith needed a ladder to get the ball out of the basket every time a team scored!

Since then, basketball has become a favorite sport. And in 1997, the world of basketball took a big step forward when the Women's National Basketball Association (WNBA) was started.

(Continued)

Women's and men's basketball games follow most of the same rules. Each team has five players on the court. They dribble and pass the ball down the court to shoot baskets. Different kinds of baskets earn different points.

Depending on where the player is standing when making the shot, a shot can be worth one point, two points, or three points.

❖❖❖❖❖❖ ❖❖❖❖❖❖ ❖❖❖❖❖❖ ❖❖❖❖❖❖ ❖❖❖❖❖❖ ❖❖❖❖❖❖ ❖❖❖❖❖❖ ❖❖❖❖❖❖

TEXT SAMPLES

Rainwalkers

In my family we wish for rain. Rain boots on, coats sometimes, and out the door we go. This has always been the case.

There I am, maybe seven or eight, walking up the hill with my dad. It is raining, I mean pouring, and we are out in it like two fish. Our skin is shiny in our slickers, and rain slides down our faces.

I am thrilled. We are on the job, my dad and me. Late summer, early fall and it is our last week in Vermont before we go back to Brooklyn for the year. I can tell how sad my dad feels. He isn't sure he's gotten enough fresh Vermont air in his body to float him through a year of concrete and smog. Me, I know I haven't eaten enough blueberries, swum enough times in the West River, or even gotten bitten by enough mosquitoes to feel ready to go back to East 22nd Street in Flatbush.

So here we walk, in the rain up the hill, hardly talking. We can't really hear because it is raining too hard. It doesn't matter to us. We've got work to do. Our sharp, blue eyes scan the road like the hawks we've watched circle the apple field.

We are looking for salamanders, which are amphibians, like frogs and toads. They resemble lizards but are scaleless and covered with soft, moist skin. Our first find, a pinky-sized Red Eft, stands in the middle of the road. I pick it up and move it across the road. Soon we've moved over 20 salamanders out of harm's way. I remember how cool and soft their brilliant bodies felt in my fingers. Their eyes rimmed in gold staring out at me, I remember wondering what they thought of me and my giant rough hands. And I remember one walk up the hill to the old village center when my dad and I moved 108 salamanders off the road. It was our record. I think it still stands.

Red Efts are a kids' dream come true, so small and touchable, and their tangerine color so outlandish in a world dedicated to camouflage. No teeth, fangs, claws, or quills. They are damp but not slimy, and it almost looks like they are smirking or smiling as if they've just shared a good joke.

They're poisonous to ingest but not toxic to the touch. They don't squirt slime in your hand or spray out any stench. And anybody can find them without much searching. They are bold, standing on top of mushrooms, climbing up rotting logs, their bright color announcing their presence.

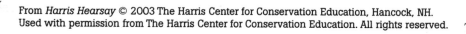

Otters Just Want to Have Fun

The otter, among all of the wild animals in New England, has a reputation for playing all of the time. It is not that the otter is irresponsible; it's just that its responsibilities are few and easily met. Although all baby animals play, few adults do. The fox and the shrew search continuously for food. The vole divides its time between eating and rebuilding its tunnels. Woodchucks and squirrels worry a great deal, and not without reason.

But the otter? Its food supply of clams, crayfish, insects, and fish is readily available. There are numerous stories of otters teasing each other by hiding food; surely it would not be treated so lightly if it were in short supply. Unlike the hare, the mouse, or the deer, the otter doesn't spend a lot of time listening for the enemy. Its only one is man, and its best defense is to slip under the surface of the water as a person comes crashing through the woods.

The otter spends absolutely no time preparing for winters. Its year-round house has doors both above and below the water, so it is ready for ice. Its coat is thick and warm, and its swimmer's webbed feet make great snowshoes. All of its spare time is devoted to perfecting its slide and its dive and other "fun" skills.

In the fresh snow it is easy for us to recognize the otter's familiar pattern of three hops and a slide. Even if there is no hill for sliding, the otter just flops down on its belly and pushes along as if it were riding a scooter.

❖❖❖❖❖❖❖ ❖❖❖❖❖❖❖ ❖❖❖❖❖❖❖ ❖❖❖❖❖❖❖ ❖❖❖❖❖❖❖ ❖❖❖❖❖❖❖ ❖❖❖❖❖❖❖ ❖❖❖❖❖❖❖

Real-World Samples With Questions

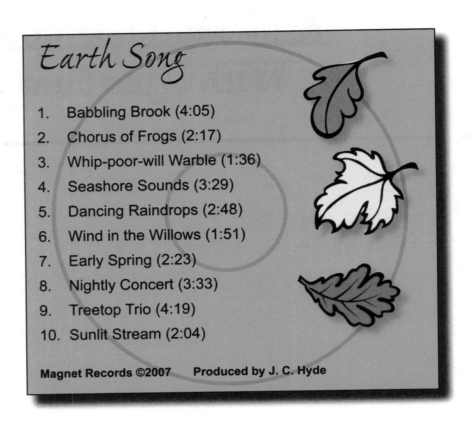

Earth Song

1. Babbling Brook (4:05)
2. Chorus of Frogs (2:17)
3. Whip-poor-will Warble (1:36)
4. Seashore Sounds (3:29)
5. Dancing Raindrops (2:48)
6. Wind in the Willows (1:51)
7. Early Spring (2:23)
8. Nightly Concert (3:33)
9. Treetop Trio (4:19)
10. Sunlit Stream (2:04)

Magnet Records ©2007   Produced by J. C. Hyde

Questions

Right There: **In what year was the CD produced?**

Think, Search, and Find: **How many songs mention some form of water in their titles?**

Author and Me: **What common theme do all the songs share?**

On My Own: **If you could create a music concert for your friends, what performers would you include?**

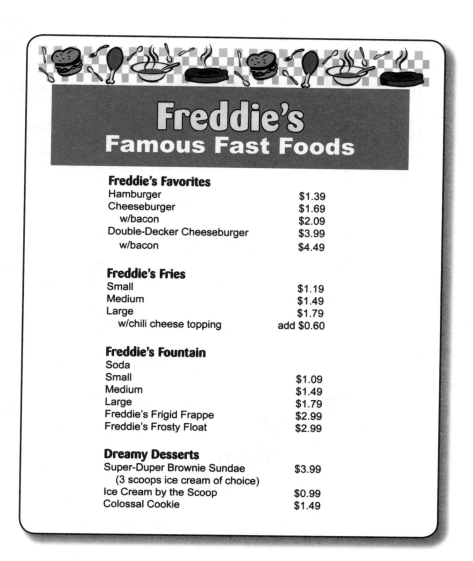

Freddie's
Famous Fast Foods

Freddie's Favorites

Hamburger	$1.39
Cheeseburger	$1.69
w/bacon	$2.09
Double-Decker Cheeseburger	$3.99
w/bacon	$4.49

Freddie's Fries

Small	$1.19
Medium	$1.49
Large	$1.79
w/chili cheese topping	add $0.60

Freddie's Fountain

Soda	
Small	$1.09
Medium	$1.49
Large	$1.79
Freddie's Frigid Frappe	$2.99
Freddie's Frosty Float	$2.99

Dreamy Desserts

Super-Duper Brownie Sundae	$3.99
(3 scoops ice cream of choice)	
Ice Cream by the Scoop	$0.99
Colossal Cookie	$1.49

Questions

Right There: **How much does a double-decker cheeseburger cost?**

Think, Search, and Find: **How many items cost less than $2.99 but more than $1.39?**

Author and Me: **If you had $5.00 to spend, what would you order?**

On My Own: **Describe your favorite place to eat out.**

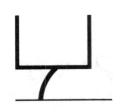

FAIRLAWN
Recreation Department

Football Schedule for September

* The team listed first is considered the visitor.
**All games are played on Saturdays at Henley Field.

Good Luck!

Have Fun!

GO TEAM GO!

Rah! Rah!

September 6
Tigers vs. Pirates   10:00 am
Bears vs. Bulldogs   2:00 pm
Panthers vs. Tornados   6:00 pm

September 13
Tornados vs. Tigers   9:00 am
Pirates vs. Bears   1:00 pm
Bulldogs vs. Panthers   5:00 pm

September 20
Panthers vs. Bears   10:00 am
Bulldogs vs. Tornados   2:00 pm
Tigers vs. Pirates   6:00 pm

September 27
Panthers vs. Tigers   9:00 am
Pirates vs. Bulldogs   1:00 pm
Bears vs. Tornados   5:00 pm

Questions

Right There: **Where are the games played?**

Think, Search, and Find: **How many times do the Pirates play the Tigers?**

Author and Me: **Why do you think there's a break between each game on Saturday?**

On My Own: **In your opinion, what sport is the most dangerous?**

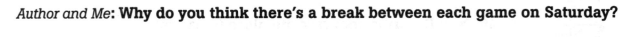

Don't forget

Chocolate chips
Eggs
Butter
Flour
Sugar-white & brown
Non-stick Cooking Spray
Vanilla
Walnuts

... the Groceries

Questions

Right There: **What kind of nuts are on the list?**

Think, Search, and Find: **How many items on the list would be found in the refrigerated section of the grocery store?**

Author and Me: **Based on the grocery list, what type of food is most likely being prepared?**

One My Own: **What is your favorite food to make? List all or some of the ingredients needed.**

Cadot Middle School

ANNOUNCEMENT

Workshop for the Model Solar Car Project

Teachers and their students can learn how to design and craft model solar electric cars using standard motors and solar panels. This interdisciplinary, hands-on project provides an excellent opportunity for students to apply skills in engineering, physical sciences, mathematics, teamwork, and problem-solving. At the same time they will learn about important energy issues. After participating in this workshop, students who are interested will be able to get involved with the region's solar car spring race—the Junior Solar Sprint. This FREE workshop is in the school cafeteria on Saturday, October 18, from 3:30 to 7:00 PM and includes a pizza dinner.

Questions

Right There: **How much does the workshop cost?**

Think, Search, and Find: **What can you learn at the workshop and what skills will you use?**

Author and Me: **What are the benefits of a solar electric car?**

On My Own: **If you could buy a car, what would it be? Explain your answer.**

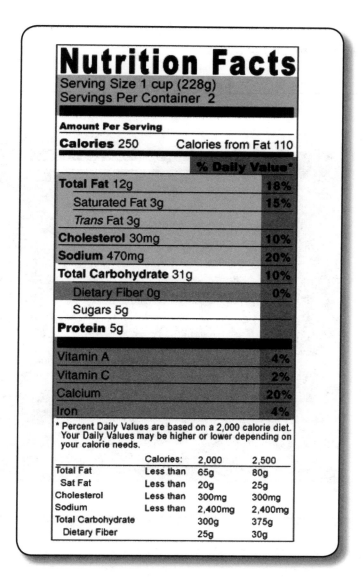

Nutrition Facts

Serving Size 1 cup (228g)
Servings Per Container 2

Amount Per Serving

Calories 250 Calories from Fat 110

	% Daily Value*
Total Fat 12g	18%
Saturated Fat 3g	15%
Trans Fat 3g	
Cholesterol 30mg	10%
Sodium 470mg	20%
Total Carbohydrate 31g	10%
Dietary Fiber 0g	0%
Sugars 5g	
Protein 5g	
Vitamin A	4%
Vitamin C	2%
Calcium	20%
Iron	4%

* Percent Daily Values are based on a 2,000 calorie diet.
Your Daily Values may be higher or lower depending on
your calorie needs.

	Calories:	2,000	2,500
Total Fat	Less than	65g	80g
Sat Fat	Less than	20g	25g
Cholesterol	Less than	300mg	300mg
Sodium	Less than	2,400mg	2,400mg
Total Carbohydrate		300g	375g
Dietary Fiber		25g	30g

Questions

Right There: **What is the serving size on this nutrition label?**

Think, Search, and Find: **Based on the % Daily Value, list the nutrients from highest to lowest percentages.**

Author and Me: **If you want to increase the amount of vitamin C, iron, and fiber in your diet, would you consider this food a good choice? Explain your answer.**

On My Own: **Do you think it's more important to pay attention to the price of an item or its nutritional value? Why?**

Temperature Map of U.S.

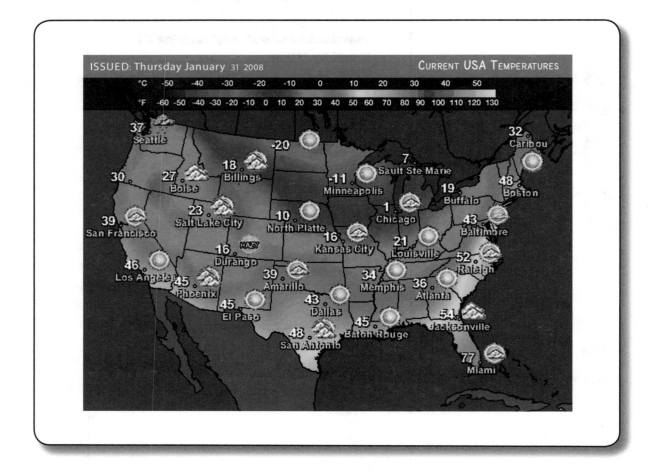

ISSUED: Thursday January 31 2008   CURRENT USA TEMPERATURES

Questions

Right There: **When was this weather map issued?**

Think, Search, and Find: **What cities had temperatures in the 30s on that day?**

Author and Me: **If you don't like cold weather, where would you prefer to live based on these temperatures?**

On My Own: **What time of year do you like the best and why?**

PARTY!

For _Scott - A Surprise Party!_

Date _Sun. Oct. 1st_   Time _3-5 pm_

Given by _His parents - Bob & Val_

Address _Party to be held at_

Grounder's Grill

R.S.V.P. _732-5681 by Sept. 1st_

Questions

Right There: **What time will the party start?**

Think, Search, and Find: **How much time is there between the RSVP date and the date of the party?**

Author and Me: **What type of food will most likely be served?**

On My Own: **What's your favorite party game to play?**

MOVIE MADNESS

~ FRIDAY ~

Ugga-Bugga World	3, 5, 7:30
The Evil Cheezit	5, 7:15, 10
The Lunch Box Mystery	12, 1:45, 4, 5:45, 8
Mabel Loves Moby	4:30, 7:30

~ SATURDAY ~

Black-Eyed Dog	3, 5, 8:10
Rainforest Rhumba	7:30, 10:15
House of Chills	1:30, 3:30, 5:30, 7:30

Questions

Right There: **What time is the first showing of "Mabel Loves Moby"?**

Think, Search, and Find: **Which movies will be shown after 7:30?**

Author and Me: **Which movie or movies sound scary?**

On My Own: **If you could make a movie about your life, what would it be called?**

Real-World Samples Without Questions

Stick-to-Your-Ribs French Toast

1 stick butter	1 cup brown sugar
2 tablespoons maple syrup	1 loaf French bread, cut into thick slices
5 eggs	1 ½ cups milk
2 teaspoons vanilla	Pinch of nutmeg

Melt butter, add brown sugar and maple syrup, and stir until sugar is dissolved. Pour into 9x13-inch baking pan. Place bread slices on top of mixture. In bowl, beat eggs, milk, vanilla, and nutmeg until well blended. Pour over bread slices, cover the pan, and refrigerate overnight. Bake uncovered at 350° for 45 minutes.

REAL-WORLD SAMPLES

August 28, 2005

Mr. Barney Piper
Candy Q Corporation
75 Sweet Treat Drive
Sugarville, ME 04000

Dear Mr. Piper:

I have been buying your candy for my grandchildren for years and have recommended it to my family and friends. Sadly, I am writing to inform you that I found a dead bug in one of your Non-Stop Cherry Suckers. Needless to say, I am quite disappointed and am unsure of whether I can continue to purchase your products.

Please advise me on how to get a refund for the price of the lollipop that I was unable to enjoy. Thank you for your time and attention to this matter.

Sincerely,

Ima Paine

Ima Paine
14 Noway Lane
Heretown, CT 06111

May 15th to October 19th

Saturdays 8:00 AM to 1:00 PM—Rain or Shine
Location: Route 116, Main Street in front of Town Office

LOCALLY MADE & ORGANICALLY GROWN:
Vegetables, Eggs, Cheese,
Maple Syrup, Homemade Baked Goods,
Strawberries & Blueberries (in season),
Apples and Cider (in season), Jams & Pickles,
Plants & Cut Flowers, Art & Fine Crafts, Herbal Products

Entertainment (10:00 AM)

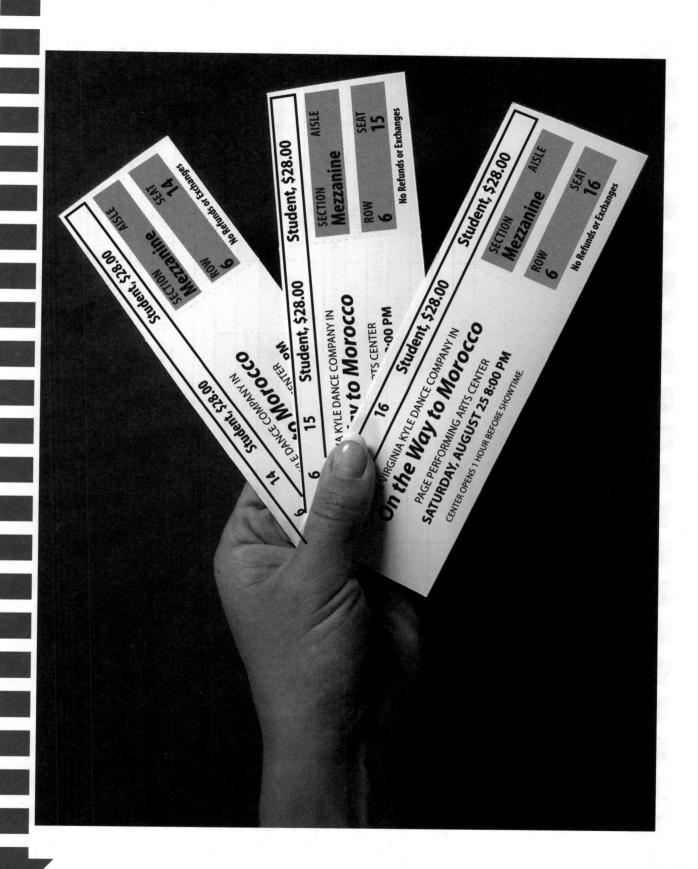

TUESDAY MORNING

Ch	7:00	8:00	9:00	10:00	11:00	12:00
2	NEWS DAY		TREE HOUSE CL.	SPARKY / ABC TV	TALK TODAY	NEWS
4	NEWS DAY	CARTOON TOWN	CRAZIES	BIG BLUE BEAR	STRAWBERRIES	NEWS
5	CARTOON CLASS.	SKIP & SAM	MOLLY MO	CHARLIE MOUSE	OSCAR	NEWS
6	PAID PROGR.	COURT / COURT	COURT / LAWMEN	COLD CASES	JUDGES	NEWS
7	THIS MORNING		THE JOEY SHOW	SALLY	THE J.D. SMITH SH.	WHO'S WHO
9	NEWS DAY		THE TALK	ENTERTAINMENT NEWS		
11	PAID PROGR.	PAID PROGR.	PAID PROGR.	PAID PROGR.	PAID PROGR.	PAID PROGR.
13	SYMPHONY IN SWEDEN		MASTER ARTISTS		17th CENTURY SCULPTURES	
TMP	CONGRESS		SENATE HEARINGS		ELECTION WEEKLY	
LOL	STAND UP	OPEN MIC	COMEDY HOUSE		OPEN MIC	LAUGH FIX
VTV	VIDEOS	MUSIC NEWS	90s AT NINE	VIDEOS	SPOTLIGHT	MUSIC NEWS
ULT	MOVIE MARATHON: WESTERNS					REVIEW IT!
KCF	ZIPPER	ABC ME / 123 TV	SING ALONG	KIDS COUNT	MAGIC CARPET	SPOT / SPOT
NBS	ON THE ICE	B.BALL GREATS	SOCCER TODAY	DRAFT / SUPERBOWL		SPORTS NEWS
GAR	HOME TIMES	HOW-TO / HOW-TO	YOU CAN DO	YARDIES	GARDEN GEAR	U DO IT / U DO IT
EAT	WILD FOOD WEEKLY		GREASY FAVS.	GRILLERS MARATHON		
ATV	DOG DAYS	CAT CARE	ANIMAL ANTICS	POLLY'S / DR. G	EXOTIC BIRDS	ANIM. ADVENTURE
CLS	BOXING HISTORY	CLASSIC B-BALL	50s / 60s	ALL-TIME H. L.	FOOTBALL FANTASTICS	

Piggy Jacks

(Eye-Hand Coordination)

This is a good activity for individuals. The player gets a single 1-inch rubber ball and 10 pigs. Piggy Jacks is played like a traditional game of jacks: Toss the ball in the air and grab 1 pig and the ball before the ball lands. Then do it again and again, picking up 1 more pig each time until all the pigs have been captured.

Piggy Banks

(Money, Addition)

This game assigns a currency value to each way a pig can land. A pig that lands on its back is worth a penny; on its side, a nickel; on all fours, a dime; and on its snout, a quarter. Each player gets 1 unmarked pig, plus pencil and paper. He rolls his pig and records the value. Then he keeps rolling—and calculating—until he reaches $1.00.

Variation: If a child's total *exceeds* a dollar, he has to start over!

Good Doggy Training School

"Every dog wants to be good."

Class Schedule:

<u>Basic Obedience Class</u> (6 weeks)
Mondays @ 6:00 PM: March 7, 14, 21, 28, April 4, 11

<u>Advanced Obedience Class</u> (4 weeks)
Wednesdays @ 6:00 PM: March 9, 16, 23, 30

<u>Recall & Stay Class</u> (3 weeks)
Saturdays @ 10:30 AM: April 2, 9, 16

<u>Tricks & Games Class</u> (2 weeks)
Fridays @ 6:00 PM: April 22, 29

<u>Walk & Train Class</u> (3 weeks)
Mondays @ 6:00 PM: May 8, 15, 22

~~~~~~~~~~~~~~~~~~

Other Services:

<u>Puppy's Personal Trainer</u>
One-on-one training in your home.

<u>Groovy Grooming</u>
The latest trends in cuts, curls, and colorations!

<u>Puppy Pedicure</u>
Keeps your pet's nails clipped—and colored, too!
Choose your favorite hue.

<u>Puppy Massage</u>
Gives your young puppy or grown dog a well-
deserved break from playing so hard all day!

**Call us today at (603) 555-1234!
We look forward to becoming
your dog's next-best friend!**

Excuses

The moose that snatched my homework
Was awfully hard to see.
He tip-toed up the stairway,
And snuck right up on me.
He demanded I relinquish
Every single page I'd done.
I put up a courageous fight,
But in the end, he won.

—Laureen Reynolds

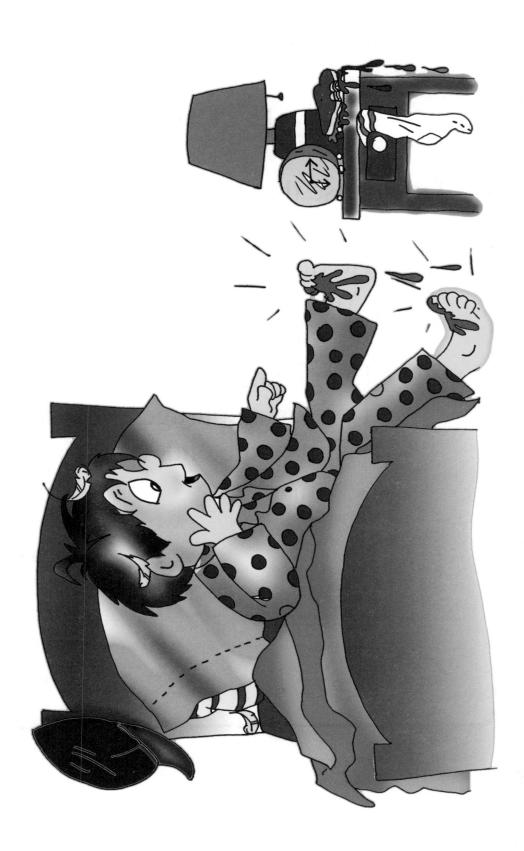

Related Citations and Recommended Reading

Cortese, E. E. "The Application of Question-Answer Relationship Strategies to Pictures." *The Reading Teacher,* 57 (4, 2003): 374–380. www.reading.org

National Assessment Governing Board. *Reading Framework for the 2009 National Assessment of Educational Progress* (Contract No. ED-02-R-0007). Washington, DC: American Institutes for Research.

Pearson, P. D., and D. D. Johnson. *Teaching Reading Comprehension.* New York: Holt, Rinehart and Winston, 1978.

Pearson, P. D., and N. K. Duke. "Comprehension Instruction in the Primary Grades," in *Comprehension Instruction: Research-Based Best Practices* ed. Cathy Collins Block and Michael Pressley, ch. 16. New York: Guilford Press, 2002.

Raphael, T. E., and K. H. Au. "QAR: Enhancing Comprehension and Test Taking Across Grades and Content Areas." *The Reading Teacher,* 59 (3, 2005): 206–221. www.reading.org

Raphael, T. E., K. H. Au, and K. Highfield. *QAR Now.* New York: Scholastic, 2006.

Raphael, T.E., and McKinney, J. (1983). An Examination of 5th and 8th Grade Children's Question-Answering Behavior: An Instructional Study in Metacognition. *Journal of Reading Behavior*, 15, 67-86.

Raphael, T. E., and Pearson, P.D. (1985). Increasing Students' Awareness of Sources of Information for Answering Questions, *American Educational Journal Research*, 22, 217-235.

Raphael, T. E. and C. A. Wonnacott. (1985). Heightening Fourth-Grade Students' Sensitivity to Sources of Information for Answering Comprehension Questions. *Reading Research Quarterly*, 20, 282-296.

There are many excellent children's books that would be good to use with older students as they learn and practice QAR. Here's a small sampling of some we recommend that are humorous and can be understood on different levels, and most have great illustrations that middle-school students will enjoy.

Bubba, The Cowboy Prince by Helen Ketteman. James Warhola, illustrator

Diary of a Worm by Doreen Cronin. Harry Bliss, illustrator

Dogzilla by Dav Pilkey

Dusty Locks and the Three Bears by Susan Lowell. Randy Cecil, illustrator

The End by David LaRochelle. Richard Egielski, illustrator

Guji Guji by Chih-Yuan Chen

Hey, Al by Arthur Yorinks. Richard Egielski, illustrator

Home on the Bayou: A Cowboy's Story by G. Brian Karas

Jumanji by Chris Van Allsburg

Kat Kong by Dav Pilkey

Martha Speaks by Susan Meddaugh

The Mud Flat Olympics by James Stevenson

The Mystery of Eatum Hall by John Kelly and Cathy Tincknell

Never Spit on Your Shoes by Denys Cazet

Oh, Brother by Arthur Yorinks. Richard Egielski, illustrator

One More Sheep by Mij Kelly and Russell Ayto

Piggie Pie! by Margie Palatini. Howard Fine, illustrator

Skippyjon Jones by Judy Schachner

Snow White in New York by Fiona French

Swine Lake by James Marshall. Maurice Sendak, illustrator

The True Story of the 3 Little Pigs! by A. Wolf (Jon Scieszka). Lane Smith, illustrator

Tub-Boo-Boo by Margie Palatini. Glin Dibley, illustrator

REPRODUCIBLES

Pointer/Signal Words

- alike
- another
- as a result
- because
- compared to
- different from
- finally
- first
- for example
- for instance

- however
- if . . . then
- in addition to
- next
- same as
- similar to
- such as
- then
- therefore
- versus

Graphic Organizer

TYPE OF QUESTION	YOUR QUESTION	YOUR ANSWER
Right There		
Think, Search, and Find		
Author and Me		
On My Own		

Question-Answer Relationships

Title _____ **Student's name** _____

QUESTIONS

In the Book/Right There _____

_____

I think this is a right-there question because _____

_____

_____

In the Book/Think, Search, and Find _____

_____

I think this is a think-search-and-find question because _____

_____

_____

In My Head/Author and Me _____

_____

I think this is an author-and-me question because _____

_____

_____

In My Head/On My Own _____

_____

I think this is an on-my-own question because _____

_____

_____

Half-Baked Questions

On My Own	Author and Me	Think, Search, and Find	Right There

INDEX

Note: *Page numbers in* italics *indicate reproducibles to be used with QAR strategy.*

Also by Betty Hollas

6 Ways to Teach the 6 Traits of Writing

Differentiating Instruction in a Whole-Group Setting, Grades 3–8

Differentiating Instruction in a Whole-Group Setting, Grades 7–12

Improve Student Behavior

Just One More Thing! (with Char Forsten & Jim Grant)

The More Ways You Teach, the More Students You Reach (with Char Forsten, Gretchen Goodman, Jim Grant & Donna Whyte)

Reducing Student Conflict with the Win–Win Way

The Top 13 Warning Signs That It's Time to Retire (with Char Forsten, Jim Grant & Donna Whyte)

Volunteers Are Vital (with Char Forsten, Jim Grant & Donna Whyte)

You Know You're a Teacher If... (with Char Forsten & Jim Grant)

Bring Betty Hollas, Char Forsten, Jim Grant, or Laureen Reynolds right to your school for on-site training! To learn how, call (877) 388-2054.